INSTRUCTOR'S MANUAL TO ACCOMPANY

Virtuous Persons, Vicious Deeds

An Introduction to Ethics

ALEXANDER E. HOOKE

Villa Julie College

MAYFIELD PUBLISHING COMPANY
MOUNTAIN VIEW, CALIFORNIA
LONDON • TORONTO

Contents

Preface		vii
Chapter 1	Why Be a Moral Person?	1
Chapter 2	How Can I Judge Moral Conduct?	16
Chapter 3	What Is Virtue Ethics	32
Chapter 4	The Whole Truth and Nothing But the Truth	43
Chapter 5	Struggling with Anger, Envy, and the Virtues	56
Chapter 6	Is It All You Need? Variations on the Love Ethic	73
Chapter 7	Self-Regarding Virtues	92
Chapter 8	Morality and the Other	108
Chapter 9	The Problems of Burdensome Lives	125
Chapter 10	Philosophy and the Good Life	140

International Standard Book Number: 0-7674-0826-8

Manufactured in the United States of America
10 9 8 7 6 5 4 3 2 1

Mayfield Publishing Company
1280 Villa Street
Mountain View, California 94041

Preface

Virtuous Persons, Vicious Deeds is designed to help introduce students
to the philosophical inquiry of morality, with special attention to
virtues and vices. Obviously no introductory course can be expected
to cover all eighty-eight selections in one semester. The organization
of topics and arrangement of selections are intended to give instructors several options in using the textbook for an introductory ethics
course. For those who are used to presenting ethics from a problems
approach, many of the selections—ranging from abortion and euthanasia to truth-telling and environmentalism—capture contemporary moral controversies. Those who prefer that an ethics course
include a variety of moral positions will find the blend of historical
and contemporary, Western and non-Western, religious and nonreligious perspectives featured in *Virtuous Persons, Vicious Deeds*
useful. Instructors who believe philosophical arguments should be
the cornerstone of an ethics course will be pleased to see many issues
in the text presented as part of an exchange or debate. In some cases,
such as the response to Sissela Bok's view on truthfulness, rejoinders
among feminists on the moral status of caring and the counter-argu-
ment to Daniel Callahan's proposals on the moral limits of treating
the elderly directly address one another. In other cases selections are
paired off according to conflicting views about whether, say, sociobiology is the answer to moral understanding, free time is a good
or bad thing for moral persons, or the moral experience begins with
the self.

Of course the most apparent emphasis in the text reflects its primary intention: to contribute to the recent revival of virtue ethics as
a central feature in thinking about the good life. Those who believe
this revival is important probably will give more weight to issues addressed in the first two chapters, then address the problems introduced
in subsequent chapters as everyday concerns to which a virtue-based
ethics has an interesting but not necessarily correct answer. For those
seeking a more sustained dialogue on this answer as the central feature
of the moral life, the first two chapters will likely serve as an important prelude to a focus on the meaning and moral value of virtues and

vices. To help you with this focus, the readings in Chapters 3 through 10 cover a range of candidates for making us virtuous or vicious. Many of the classic seven deadly sins or cardinal virtues—from pride and anger to lust, sloth, love, justice, and hope—are complemented by more recent candidates, such as care, despair, solidarity, and virtual lust.

With these different backgrounds in mind, the guides, précis, and questions that follow are intended to assist instructors in presenting the selections on their own terms as well as in the context of the chapter and the course. The multiple-choice questions are aimed for students' comprehension of key points in the selection. The discussion questions can be used to elicit students' thought on the selections in oral or written format, that is, as short answer or essay responses. These hints are, of course, not meant to be exhaustive. One of the underlying themes in moral philosophy is the nature or extent of human freedom. In recent modern moral philosophy this theme has focused on the kind of actions the agent is free to take or not take. Virtue ethics tends to shift this theme to concern about the kind of person a moral agent wants to become. In this spirit of free inquiry we anticipate still other ways of teaching many of the eighty-eight readings included. As with the reading and critical questions listed in *Virtuous Persons, Vicious Deeds,* the discussion and multiple-choice items offered in the instructor's manual are tools to contribute to a student's basic comprehension of key points and a philosophical appreciation of moral ideas.

Finally, a note on the selections themselves. Many are by well-known thinkers, part of the standard repertoire in introductory ethics. Others are less known, perhaps appearing for the first time in an ethics reader. Some were selected for their ability to articulate difficult thinkers or ideas; others for their wit and humor. Still others were picked for their insight into current issues, and some for their careful efforts in using virtue ethics to understand contemporary moral problems. In any case, they are included here because I believe they have something valuable to say to today's students who are interested in morality and the good life.

Chapter 1
Why Be a Moral Person?

The readings in this chapter address some popular orientations to morality. The case study begins with a student's observation of a student who can get an "A" in an ethics course while behaving immorally outside class. Then several issues are raised. Perhaps the most common issue has to do with ethical relativism, usually illustrated in the various customs and values embraced in different cultures or generations. The essays by Sumner and Garrett clarify this issue. Another popular attitude toward the moral life is couched in terms of biological or genetic factors. Are humans selfish or altruistic by nature? This question is addressed by Wilson and Mackie. Perhaps the most familiar context for moral life is religion. Selections from the Bible and Chuang Tzu elucidate two views of morality in a religious context. Still others think the central moral dilemma consists of whether one first favors oneself or another. To distinguish how this dilemma involves both a question of human nature and one of human morality, the selections by Browne and Noddings discuss whether the primary moral experience of individuals is of the detached self or the self-in-relation.

If an instructor is intrigued by the metaethical or human nature questions about morality, some coverage of the ideas raised in all the readings is worth pursuing. An instructor who is more interested in the philosophical issues that underlie moral thought might assign one or two pairs of readings in addition to the case study. The relation between genetics and moral conduct has been a lively issue in recent years. Most students probably have a rough sense of cultural relativism and the religious tradition. And nearly every student is familiar with the egoist's claim that one should do whatever is right for oneself, as long as no one else is being harmed. If you want to investigate these issues carefully, at least two weeks could be devoted to this chapter. If you are eager to get to the virtues and vices, you might assign the case study and then highlight one or two of the issues, summarizing or skipping the others.

1. Case Study: Robert Coles, "The Disparity between Intellect and Character"

Coles recounts an episode brought to his attention by one of his students. She asked him what the point to an ethics course is. A student can get an "A" in the course but outside the classroom behave immorally. She points out the disappointing experience she had with one of those students who made rather insulting advances toward her. This experience parallels that of anyone who is expected to teach morality, from instructors to religious leaders to politicians. The disparity between what one says and what one does is a recurring theme for all moral students.

Multiple-Choice Questions

1. Coles's discussion focuses on a student who is bothered by another student who gets an "A" in an ethics course, yet outside the classroom the student discovers
   a. he is selling drugs to residents in the college dorm.
   *b. he makes unwanted sexual advances to the student.
   c. he harasses the student about helping him cheat on a final exam.
   d. he is hacking into the college computer network to get access to information about fellow students.

2. Coles responds to the student's concerns by
   a. finding the student and changing his grade from an "A" to a "D."
   b. resigning his job as an instructor of ethics.
   c. telling the student that she should call the college dean or provost and lodge a formal complaint against the male student.
   *d. reconsidering the primary task of teaching ethics.

Discussion Questions

1. Are intelligent people moral? Are moral people intelligent? Consider examples of moral persons in history, the movies, or in novels. Do you believe they were or are moral based on their actions, the results of their actions, or their character?

2

2. Can moral character be taught, or is it something that one is born with? If it is taught, who are the best teachers? In most areas of life, from jobs to hobbies and sports, people are trained by experts, specialists, or coaches. Can people be taught by moral trainers?

2. William Graham Sumner, "Folkways"

This is a classic statement on ethical relativism. Sumner describes a variety of cultural traditions and customs while interweaving them with the larger issue of their purpose. Usually students are aware of some strange customs and tend to express a tolerance of them, as long as the customs do not get exported to the United States. The philosophical disputes on ethical and cultural relativism are not that simple, of course. From the excerpts included, Sumner argues that folkways have a practical and essential origin: to provide for all members of a society the needs of life. Gradually the folkways become part of tradition and are followed even if they are not understood. They become ingrained in the unconscious of a society's members. They take on the status of true, sacred, or absolute. To ignore or violate a folkway is akin to disgracing a culture's ancient ancestors, disobeying the gods, or disrupting the social order.

Sumner acknowledges that many folkways can be harmful to individuals. And from an outsider's point of view many folkways seem irrational in that they are not founded on common sense or recognizable facts. From an insider's perspective, there is a logic to the folkways insofar as they are coherent and effective in organizing and sustaining a society. More simply, for an insider folkways are true or good whereas another culture's folkways are false or bad. According to Sumner, when folkways develop into doctrines of welfare, they are considered mores. Mores are generalizations of the smaller truths that form folkways. The taboo of eating a certain food becomes a more, for example, when it is couched in terms of sacred rules or social laws. Anthropologist Marvin Harris's work on cultural attitudes on food is in part an updated version of Sumner's distinction. In Harris's view, the taboo on eating cows in India began as a practical device. Cows were valuable for providing milk and working on the farm. To kill a cow simply for its tasty flesh was an indulgence that could not be excused for now the services of the cow were permanently lost. Hence, according to Harris, this folkway gradually became a more when the taboo took on a religious and ethical position that the cow was sacred. Analogous cases could be made in the United States for its taboos on eating cats and dogs.

Multiple-Choice Questions

1. Which one of the following is NOT used to have individuals follow and respect the folkways?
   a. infliction of pain
   b. learning the right habits at an early age
   *c. democratic vote by all members who passed puberty rituals
   d. fear of angry ghosts and ancestors

2. For Sumner immorality means
   a. a violation of human rights.
   b. obedience to the mores of a particular culture.
   c. pursuing pleasure without consulting an ethics teacher.
   *d. anything that is contrary to the mores of a particular culture.

3. The evil attributed to camels by the Yakuts is an example of a folkway that
   *a. begins by accident or superstition.
   b. is supported by biological evidence that camels should not live too close to people.
   c. begins by a general consensus among a culture's educated elite.
   d. has rational grounds for acceptance by the culture.

Discussion Questions

1. That people may experience pain by following a folkway is not necessarily an argument that the folkway is bad. What is the general purpose of folkways, customs, and mores? Is it important that people respect and obey the customs even if they do not understand them?

2. Imagine college or university life as a small society. Which rules or codes of conduct could be understood from the perspective of Sumner? Are the rules or codes efficient? Do they provide for the needs of the college and as many of its members as possible? Are there any folkways of college life that seem superstitious, inefficient, outdated, or contrary to individual pursuits? Explain your examples.

3. Sumner observes that folkways do change. How do they change? Can you think of a folkway in your life that has changed in your lifetime? Briefly clarify the folkway and possible reasons for its change.

3. Richard Garrett, "Dilemma's Case for Ethical Relativism"

If the Sumner essay seems too remote or if you prefer brief coverage of ethical relativism, the dialogue by Richard Garrett might suffice. He is fair in presenting the major points of cultural variations and their relevance to ethics. Moreover, he has the participants, Dilemma, Siddhartha, Max, and Homer speaking in relatively jargon-free language.

The dialogue begins with Max citing a case of an African tribe called the Ikes. (This likely derives from Colin Turnbull's study of the Ik in *The Mountain People*.) They were suffering from drought and reduced to conditions in which, as described by one observer, a son would steal food from his father. Yet on what basis can we make moral judgments? With this question most of the dialogue is between Dilemma's defense of relativism and Siddhartha's challenge. One of the arguments involves the analogy between progress in other fields, such as medicine, and progress in moral thought. Dilemma thinks any analogy between moral thought and the scientific inquiry of other disciplines is inadequate because moral thought cannot agree on basic facts. Siddhartha then questions Dilemma's view of inquiry by noting the importance—and universal value—of rational discourse.

Multiple-Choice Questions

1. Siddartha raises the analogy of the shape of the earth to show that
   a. no one can agree on its shape, just as no one can agree on the single correct morality.
   b. scientists should have more influence in moral discussions.
   *c. just as people can be wrong about the world being a pyramid, they can be wrong about a specific moral belief.
   d. both scientific and moral beliefs are subject to religious and political dictates.

2. Siddartha cites the ending of slavery in the United States as a sign of moral progress. Dilemma responds by pointing out that this event is a sign not of progress but of
    *a. a recognition that American society was living in contradiction to its own principles.
    b. a recognition that American society was losing international respect and would suffer economically from trade embargoes.
    c. the misfortune of the South in losing the Civil War.
    d. the good fortune of the North in keeping the country united; ending slavery was only a side effect.

3. Siddartha concludes that three universal wrongs are
    a. murder, dishonesty, and adultery.
    b. thievery, dishonesty, and computer hacking.
    *c. dishonesty, murder, and thievery.
    d. thievery, selfishness, and watching the Jerry Springer Show.

Discussion Questions

1. Which of the speakers in the dialogue do you agree with? Why? Is there a winner?

2. Does Siddhartha give a sufficient case to refute Dilemma's position? How might Dilemma respond to the concluding points?

3. Several analogies are given to highlight the possibility of progress or universality in moral beliefs. Can you devise your own analogy to either support or weaken this possibility?

4. E. O. Wilson, "The Morality of the Gene"

One of the leading proponents of sociobiology, E. O. Wilson suggests in this selection that moral philosophers should suspend their discussion about right and wrong and listen for a moment to researchers from a more scientific background. Specifically, from a Darwinist perspective the individual's own well-being is not the center of its essential purposes. As long as moral thinkers focus on the good for individuals, according to Wilson, they will poorly estimate the role of moral conduct.

Wilson begins with Albert Camus's famous declaration that the only serious philosophical issue is whether one should commit suicide in light of a world in which things are generally absurd—i.e., humans do not have any evident meaningful place in the scheme of things. The problem with Camus's outlook is characteristic of much moral philosophy. It places too much weight on self-consciousness. From a biological perspective, however, the primary function of an organism is to be a temporary carrier of the genes that will sustain and improve the species. Hence the gene is in fact altruistic. From this biological basis we can better understand the functions of moral principles and values as tools to direct the organisms toward their natural purposes. Social groups, kinships, and cooperative structures are meant to reinforce the efforts toward these purposes. If done properly, then, moral development is not an independent humanistic or religious inquiry but a derivative of biology.

Although Wilson tries to write for a general academic audience, some of the material is still fairly technical in terms of biological and genetic descriptions.

Multiple-Choice Questions

1. The best answer to the question, How is altruism passed on from one age to the next? is:
    a. by religious saints, for they taught the best lessons about loving your neighbor.
    b. in a brain malfunction because it is one of those annoying genes that cleverly passes itself on.
    c. through coercive commands or laws, which are needed to counter the basic selfish drives of human beings.
    *d. in kinship, in which altruistic genes seek mating with other altruistic genes, thus spreading altruism through the gene pool.

2. According to Wilson, sociobiology is defined as the systematic study of
    a. the social construction of the main ideas of the biological sciences.
    *b. the biological basis of all social behavior.
    c. the biological basis of some but not all social behavior.
    d. the biological basis of animal group behavior but not human group behavior.

3. Wilson proposes that the time has come for ethics to escape philosophers and become biologicized. Those who should consider this shift are
   a. Nobel prize winners and political leaders.
   b. medical doctors and HMOs.
   *c. humanists and scientists.
   d. scientists and New Age spiritualists.

Discussion Questions

1. What do you think moral responsibility means in the ethics of sociobiology? That is, who or what deserves moral credit or blame?

2. Can only another biologist or sociologist refute Wilson's claims? In other words, are most moral persons at best observers rather than participants in this debate?

5. J. L. Mackie, "The Law of the Jungle: Moral Alternatives and Principles of Evolution"

This essay is a response to the position of another scientist, Richard Dawes, who also supports a genetic basis for understanding ethics. Mackie reviews Dawes's book, *The Selfish Gene,* appreciating its main arguments while questioning its central thesis.

Mackie begins by describing the meaning behind the law of the jungle. He then discusses Dawes's explanation that the genes' being selfish lies in their altruism. The overall effort is to show how Dawes's hypothetical genotypes found in humans—the Cheater, the Sucker, and the Grudger—do not necessarily lead to a conclusion that biology supplants ethics as a way of understanding human good. Part of Mackie's argument is that if the world had only one pair of these genotypes the species would either stabilize or wipe itself out. But only with the Grudger as personified by the "reciprocral altruist"—most normal people, Mackie implies—does the species stand a chance of improving itself. The Grudger is also a moral agent, one for whom moral reflection and decisions are part of life. For Mackie, then, to the extent that the moral agent is human, the biological perspective does not supplant ethics.

As with the Wilson selection, this does contain some technical language. You might address this issue by going over both essays carefully, or assigning an excerpt from either essay and summarizing the overall arguments. Part of the decision may lie in your estimation of your students' reading ability. In light of recent controversies about cloning, genetic engineering, and genetic accounts that explain a range of human life forms from homosexuality to shyness and kleptomania, the issues raised by the Wilson and Mackie selections are quite current.

Multiple-Choice Questions

1. In the grooming analogy, the Sucker is
   a. one who tries to cheat but fails.
   b. one who grooms only those who are morally deserving.
   *c. one who grooms anyone who needs it.
   d. one who grooms those who promise to pay for the services but do not.

2. A Grudger is
   *a. rather like you and me.
   b. someone who enjoys hating other individuals.
   c. an angry person waiting to explode.
   d. the kind of person who appears as a guest on talk shows to embarrass his friends or family.

Discussion Questions

1. Can you think of any current or historical examples of Cheaters, Suckers, or Grudgers? Consider your readings in other classes, personal experiences, or favorite movies or television shows.

2. Do you think the Cheaters/Suckers/Grudgers distinctions are about different groups of people or about three attitudes that we all have experienced in ourselves? On what passage do you base your answer?

3. If you do a good or bad deed, should you praise or blame your biological parents?

6. Selections from "The Holy Bible: Ten Commandments, Beatitudes, and Parables"

Many students are familiar with the creationist/evolutionist debate, even if on superficial terms. But they may not always be aware of the moral implications in that debate. One way of helping them with a richer understanding of this debate is by juxtaposing the sociobiological dispute with a traditional religious perspective.

The selections from the Bible express a portion of one such perspective. Of course, the idea that there is a monolithic or inherently consistent Judeo-Christian morality is more myth than fact. Still, some of the outstanding features are captured in the Ten Commandments, some of which still underlie the moral basis of modern democracy. The so-called love ethic that is illustrated in the Beatitudes represents a different kind of moral challenge, one that only saints can fully meet. The parables, especially the one on the rich, evoke some of the subtleties of the religious perspective.

All of the selections can stand on their own. So it is a judgment call regarding which selections might be assigned.

Multiple-Choice Questions

1. In the Commandment on respecting the Sabbath, the ones who should NOT work include
   a. family members and slaves, but not animals.
   *b. family members, slaves, and animals.
   c. family members and animals, but not slaves.
   d. family members, slaves, animals, but not cashiers at 7-Eleven.

2. In the selection from Romans, the mind is a slave to the law of God as the flesh is a slave to
   a. the law of cultural mores.
   b. the temptations of Satan.
   *c. the law of sin.
   d. the enticements of advertising.

3. According to Jesus, one who has obeyed the commandments but is wealthy should
   a. give money to others who do not sin.
   *b. give money to the poor.

c.   sell one's possessions and give the money to one's
     children.

d.   donate all extra money to one's church.

Discussion Questions

1.   Do any of the selections from the Bible promise worldly happi-
     ness as part of the moral life?

2.   Is there an implicit view of human nature in the biblical selec-
     tions? Briefly illustrate your answer.

3.   Which contemporary moral attitudes do you see as an extension
     of biblical morality and which do you see as contrary? Be
     specific.

7. Chuang Tzu, "Let It Be: Meditations on Tao and Freedom"

Another traditional religious ethic is expressed in Chuang Tzu's version of Taoism. Like the Bible, Chuang Tzu's writings often take the
form of parables, some straightforward, others witty or paradoxical.
Though these parables do not take the form of arguments in the conventional sense, they often introduce ideas that are recurring for those
interested in moral thought.

Again, the selections here can probably be assigned piecemeal,
depending on your focus and sense for student interests. Many of the
stories highlight the possible usefulness or uselessness of spoken words
in capturing the good life. Others emphasize the importance of clarity,
though the stories on clarity are not always so clear. In assigning the
selections, an instructor might keep in mind Chuang Tzu's sense of
happiness, for that will help in addressing the "why be moral"
question.

Multiple-Choice Questions

1.   In proclaiming "Let it be!" Chuang Tzu is
     *a.   celebrating the ordinary elements of everyday life.
     b.   lamenting the miseries of human life.
     c.   warning us about the futility of revolutionary change.
     d.   working on the Chinese translation of a Beatles song.

2. In the section "Supreme Happiness," the best means to reaching happiness is through
   a. working hard at one's hobbies and personal interests.
   b. obtaining sufficient wealth so that you don't have to take orders from others.
   *c. inaction, insofar as this is the way toward realizing peace.
   d. activity based on one's socially recognized talents.

3. Advising Yen Ho on tutoring an unvirtuous prince, Chu Po-yu encourages the ideal of harmonizing. Hence, if the prince beings acting like a child, the tutor should
   a. act like a baby.
   *b. act like a child.
   c. act like a parent.
   d. act like an animal.

Discussion Questions

1. How is the Way a central feature of Chuang Tzu's outlook?

2. What is the distinct, even paradoxical, feature of words in his discussion? Does the wise or moral person avoid or require words in order to gain perfection?

8. Harry Browne, "The Unselfishness Trap"

This piece appears in many ethics anthologies. Browne clearly presents the case for ethical egoism while questioning the usefulness of altruistic principles. His analogies and examples are accessible to introductory students. Moreover, Browne provides a rationale for what many people intuitively believe: Morality is about happiness, and only I know what makes me happy.

The argument is straightforward. Browne observes how unselfish behavior does not really make for a happier world. Worse, altruism ignores a fact of reality—people are basically selfish. He then offers two worlds. One world directs people to act on behalf of others, even if they do not want to. The second world directs people to act on their own interests, which is a more honest approach. From Browne's portrayal of the worlds, a rational person who believes worldly happiness is the chief aim of moral life will choose the second world. In this world social interaction is not geared toward benefiting others. It is based on achieving long-term self-interests.

12

Multiple-Choice Questions

1. In the example of his landlady giving Browne a piece of freshly baked cake, the landlady
   a. actually harmed Browne because he is allergic to sugar.
   *b. presumed to know what Browne likes.
   c. actually was being selfish because she wanted Browne to paint the apartment.
   d. was scheming because she was romantically interested in Browne and thought chocolate cake was a good start.

2. Which activity is NOT part of the unselfishness trap?
   a. regretfully paying for an aunt's surgery after you saved money for a new car
   b. being required to have your tax money go to the poor
   *c. taking out half of your savings to help a neighbor who said he changed his will to include you as one of his heirs
   d. passing a ball around because you feel guilty enjoying it

Discussion Questions

1. How does Browne define happiness? Do you agree with his definition? Can you offer a different version of happiness? Which components does your version include that Browne's does not?

2. Do you accept his claim that everyone is selfish? Carefully look at his defense of this claim. Does he use the term "selfish" consistently and accurately? Look at specific passages.

9. Nel Noddings, "Relational Virtues"

One of the leading feminist writers on ethics, Noddings questions the egoist position here by addressing the idea of the detached or isolated self. This focus is a way of circumventing the selfish/unselfish tension that ethical egoists thrive on in order to show that altruistic behavior is invariably selfish. A consequence of her position is an ethic of care, which is elaborated in Chapter 8.

The selection here raises a number of examples to highlight a fact ignored by egoists. We always find ourselves in a relation with someone else. Whether as friend with friend, student with teacher, child with parent, colleague with colleague, moral thought and conduct begins with the self-in-relation. For Noddings, then, the self as autonomous or detached is not the basic ontological condition of humans. Egoists forget this. Unfortunately, in her view, popular images of successful people celebrate those who have so much that they seem not to need anyone: Lee Iacocca, business tycoon, rather than Atticus Finch, from *To Kill a Mockingbird*.

Noddings completes the chapter by returning us to the question of moral pedagogy.

Multiple-Choice Questions

1. Which people have exemplified the self-in-relation throughout history?
   a. men and women in non-Western cultures
   b. only females who have been mothers
   *c. most women
   d. women who have been raised in a religious environment

2. Education can help students and society with moral guidance by encouraging
   a. students to treat school work as a forerunner to a successful career.
   b. students to go to graduate school so they can earn a better and more stable living.
   *c. moderation, such as redistributing the wealth.
   d. self-esteem, so we all feel better about ourselves.

Discussion Questions

1. Many social theorists think conflict is essential to human existence. How do you think Noddings understands conflict? Is it part of or contrary to the self-in-relation?

2. Periodically magazines, newspapers, or television report a new survey of the most admired men and women in the United States or in the world. Is Noddings correct that those at the top reflect admiration for power and wealth? Who would you put at the top?

Chapter Review Questions

1. The case study by Robert Coles highlights a moral drama among two students. Which of the readings in the chapter do you think best supports the young woman who presented her concerns to Coles? Which of the readings best supports the young man? In developing your answer, keep in mind how support can be viewed as an explanation or as a justification.

2. Of the readings covered in Chapter 1, which one (or two) reflect the moral beliefs you learned as a child, teenager, or student? Do these beliefs largely stem from family life, school life, or popular entertainment, religion, or some other source? In developing your answer, consider which reading presents a moral approach most foreign or opposed to your beliefs. Be specific in your answer.

3. Where do you stand on moral relativism and ethical egoism? Can you be both a cultural relativist and a moralist who stresses the pursuit of selfish happiness? Select two or three readings to support your response.

Chapter 2
How Can I Judge Moral Conduct?

The perspectives highlighting this chapter are quite familiar. Somehow it does not seem an ethics course unless students are at least introduced to the ethical theories of deontology and utilitarianism, invariably represented by Kant and Bentham or Mill. Moreover, since both perspectives portray their adherents as supporting a true moral theory, it is hard to avoid addressing students' reservations about the status of moral judgments. Are these judgments true or false, or are they an expression of an attitude or personal preference? On what basis, to put it in analytical terms, is a moral judgment a meaningful statement about the world?

Being introduced to this chapter by Lingis's case study about torture, students have the chance to read about a current phenomenon that for them likely sparks a moral judgment. The reasons behind moral judgments are addressed by the subsequent selections. Nagel provides a lucid account for the objective basis of moral judgments. Bentham's hedonic calculus is a good summation of one objective account of moral thought. It contrasts nicely with Kant's alternative to an ethical belief that is based on pleasure and pain. The difficulty of reading Bentham or Kant for introductory students should not be understated. To help them I have included two thoughtful and clearly presented essays by Rachels and Stelmach. Each outlines the coherence of the main ideas of the moral theory and closes with a thoughtful challenge to the theory. De Beauvoir and Lao Tzu close out this chapter with their respective views on the recurring efforts of humans to devise a morality that is both universal and practical for everyday dilemmas.

Depending on your objectives for the course, the readings in this chapter can be handled in several ways. If you want to focus on the philosophical dimensions of moral thought, all the readings could be given careful attention; this is the only chapter in which every writer can be safely and accurately identified as a philosopher. This identity may not mean a whole lot to an average introductory student, but in many teaching situations ethics is the only philosophy course a student will take. The readings here discuss both the value of philosophy and the importance of moral thinking.

For those interested in sustaining some of the discussions from Chapter 1, Nagel, Bentham, and Kant are obvious responses to ethical relativism. De Beauvoir and Lao Tzu are useful in questioning the ideas raised in either the biological or religious codifications of morality. If you want to interest students about the issues of human nature presumed by moral beliefs, then you might correlate the selections in Chapter 2 with those in Chapter 1. For example, Browne's view on egoism might be followed up with discussions by Rachels or Stelmach.

If you are eager to concentrate on virtues and vices, Lingis's case study might be followed by selections about social utility, rationality, and the moral value of free choice and ambiguity. Pointing out the limitations of these theories can then set up the attention to virtue ethics as a basis for moral judgment. Of course, as your course unfolds and if students find difficulties with a virtue-based ethics, you may want to revive the study of deontology or utilitarianism.

10. Case Study: Alphonso Lingis, "A Doctor in Havana"

This essay has two distinct components. First Lingis outlines different kinds of speech, then he distinguishes frivolous speech from serious speech. Serious speech involves philosophical efforts in discussing the truth, but it also has a special relation to speaking on behalf of those who are silent or being silenced, such as those who are tortured. Torture, observes Lingis, is not a cruelty waged by barbarians. It is an exercise practiced in civilized and rational communities. In the second part Lingis cites an extended report of two women from South America who were victims to an ingenious torture by members of the military regime in Brazil. Their faces were horribly rearranged so that they barely resembled human beings. Yet the women refused to give up the fight for political justice. "No one will ever silence me," one of them promises.

Lingis's writing is relatively free of philosophical terminology, and his vocabulary is rich. His style also relies on juxtapositions that encourage readers to consider their own beliefs when discovering the experiences and thoughts of others. As with many selections, it might be useful to begin the meeting on Lingis's essay by going over some new words.

Multiple-Choice Questions

1. Which one of the following is NOT mentioned as a contemporary example of tortured silence?
   a. 40,000 children dying each day in slums
   b. AIDS victims
   *c. victims of dysfunctional families
   d. Quechua peasants

2. When one speaks seriously, observes Lingis, one
   a. expects the listener to remember the essential aspects of the argument.
   b. hides emotions so that only the rational points are communicated.
   c. participates in the universal dialogue best exemplified in college seminars.
   *d. speaks for the silent and silenced.

3. According to Luis, the plastic surgeon, the torturers removed all the teeth of one woman and replaced them with
   a. a set of brittle wooden teeth, to prevent any comfort in eating.
   *b. two dog incisors.
   c. nothing, so that she would be ashamed to eat or laugh.
   d. her own teeth but rearranged so that the molars were in the front.

Discussion Questions

1. What are the different kinds of speech introduced by Lingis? Which effect, purpose, or value does each have? In your own life—such as at work, in college, going to a party or out on a date—do you recognize these kinds of speech? Do you think they have the same effect as suggested by Lingis—for example, that some forms of speech are frivolous whereas others are meant to ignore or respond to others? Which passages support your answer?

2. After reading the report of the two women tortured in Brazil, do you think there is a moral good or evil in their experiences or the lives of the perpetrators? Is your answer to this based on
   a. your personal taste or preference?
   b. an instinctively human sense of right and wrong?

c. a learned response, the result of years of successful social conditioning by your parents?

d. a learned response that resulted from a momentary but successful biological coupling of your genetic ancestors?

e. your belief in the everyday practice of the golden rule?

f. beliefs that every rational person can and should agree to be true?

g. other factors?

Select the best answer and explain your reasons for picking it. You might also consider whether you think most people would answer the same as you and why (this could help in clarifying the reasons for your own answer).

11. Thomas Nagel, "The Objective Basis of Morality"

Nagel also tries to avoid philosophical terminology while presenting interesting philosophical thoughts about issues central to ethics. Here he offers a lucid account on the argument about the objectivity of moral thought and discussion. Like a patient teacher, he leads the reader through seemingly obvious examples of right and wrong, then introduces the skeptic's or relativist's objections. Nagel's rejoinders eventually lead to a deeper sense of the relativist's objections and his own position on the importance of reason in morality. That we demand consistency and reason from someone who has harmed another—"why did you do that?"—tells us that there is an objective basis in morality.

Nagel is one of the best formulators of this argument, in part because of his ability to present a complex argument so concisely. In terms of their respective backgrounds, Nagel (an American who has adopted the Anglo-American tradition in philosophy) and Lingis (an American who embraces much of the Continental approach to philosophy) are a stark contrast. Yet this need not prevent students from recognizing how they address similar issues. For example, Nagel readily acknowledges that "there is no substitute for a direct concern for other people as the basis of morality." But he doubts that everyone shares this concern, and those who don't need to be persuaded with reasons. Nagel also admits that people have powerful selfish motives, which contrasts with Lingis's presentation of individuals who seldom evoke a sense of selfish interests. In any event, the separations in academic philosophy need not be perpetrated among introductory students.

They can learn from both and discover some of the diverse ways of engaging in philosophical thought.

Multiple-Choice Questions

1. The ideas of right and wrong and the ideas about obeying the rules are
   a. interchangeable.
   *b. different.
   c. linguistically different but intellectually interchangeable.
   d. legally different but morally the same.

2. An indicator that a moral judgment is more than liking or not liking an action, such as having your umbrella stolen, is
   a. the anger you have when getting caught in the rain without an umbrella.
   b. when you call your legislator to demand harsher punishment for umbrella thieves.
   *c. your resenting the thief for his or her inconsiderate motives.
   d. imaginary, because losing an umbrella to a thief is no different in terms of suffering than stubbing a toe against a rock.

3. For Nagel moral argument appeals to an impartial motivation that is supposed to be in
   *a. all of us.
   b. educated people.
   c. those brought up in Western European literature and history.
   d. all those victimized by umbrella thieves.

Discussion Questions

1. How does Nagel distinguish two kinds of relativity? Do you agree or disagree with his argument that the very capacity, expectation, or right to criticize other cultural standards as well as our own implies a common acceptance of the rational or objective basis of morality? Devise your own illustration to support your view of Nagel's position.

2. Central to Nagel's thinking is the relation between impartial and selfish motivation. He acknowledges that the latter is a powerful rival to the impartial motive. In your view, why does Nagel believe the impartial view can still win in controlling our behav-

ior? Do you accept his view? In answering, you might consider one or two of the selections from Chapter 1, such as those on the selfish gene, happiness, or self-in-relation.

12. Jeremy Bentham, "Hedonic Calculus"

This selection is often used, and for good reason. Though many think ethical relativism is the position of most undergraduates, there is good reason to think that today's youth are not much different from the youth Plato or Augustine were thinking of. In which case the moral question is not, What's wrong with relativism? but What's wrong with pleasure?

In an earlier version of this text I placed the Bentham selection with those on relativism; social utility can be relative, I figured. Reviewers caught this flaw by emphasizing the objective value of pleasure (and pain) in Bentham's thinking.

To give some background to this thinking I have also included the chapter that immediately precedes the famous chapter with the hedonic calculus. Bentham's observations on four aspects of pain and pleasure—physical, political, moral or popular, and religious—set up his general case about the responsibilities of a good legislator. In making and enforcing the rules and laws, the legislator needs to consider all four aspects in order to bring about the greatest good for the greatest number.

Depending on your students and your own emphasis in ethics, the two chapters can but need not be read together. If you like to focus on the social dimensions of ethics or think your students are interested in the philosophical connection between the hedonic calculus and the discussion on the four sources and sanctions of pleasure and pain, assigning both chapters may be useful. Bentham is not very easy reading, and covering only the passages on the seven components might be enough if you want to give more attention to other themes in the course. In either event, you might highlight the influence of utilitarian thinking because the revival of virtue ethics is in part a response to it.

Multiple-Choice Questions

1. Which is NOT considered a source or sanction of pleasure and pain?
   a. political
   b. religious

*c. financial
d. physical

2. If you are using "purity" as a consideration for eating a veggie burger for lunch, you are
   a. worried that all the ingredients are organically grown and harvested.
   b. concerned about the ingredients of the condiments to make the burger tastier.
   c. weighing if you will experience the same pleasure the next time you eat a veggie burger.
   *d. concerned that the immediate pleasure of biting into a veggie burger will be followed by disgust or pain.

3. If you are thinking about drinking lots of beer tonight and weigh the "extent" factor, you will
   a. calculate how many hours you will be enjoying the party.
   b. recount how much you have tolerated in the past so that you won't suffer a hangover.
   *c. take into account others who will enjoy or suffer the effects of your drinking.
   d. see if you can emulate Socrates and drink everyone else under the table.

Discussion Questions

1. Do you think those who make the rules—whether on a national level or in a local setting—think along utilitarian lines? Or do you feel the basis of at least some of the rules are not directed to the greatest pleasure for the greatest number of people in the community? What evidence can you offer to support your answers?

2. Many commentators distinguish rule utilitarianism from act utilitarianism. Though Bentham stresses the role of the legislator, much of his discussion addresses the importance of using the calculus for ordinary actions. Do individuals conduct themselves according to some version of the hedonic calculus? Should they? Why, or why not?

13. James Rachels, "The Debate over Utilitarianism"

Despite the enduring features of utilitarianism—particularly its linking morality with worldly happiness—it is also a favorite target for ethics teachers. It does not address the equal distribution of pleasure, it can justify using people as a means for the majority's well-being, it appeals to the baser elements of human goodness—these are some of the standard charges utilitarianism cannot answer. James Rachels articulates some of the standard criticisms and shows how a rational person can defend utilitarianism as a moral theory.

First, Rachels detaches hedonism from happiness, contending that the pursuit of pleasure distorts the fundamental sense of the good endorsed by utilitarians. Second, he clarifies the point about utilitarianism's alleged neglect of justice or fairness and whether consequences are essential to the merits of a moral theory. Then he shows how the value of rights, deceiving or mistreating other people, or breaking one's promises are central considerations for those who endorse the greatest happiness principle. Third, he revives the significance of act utilitarianism as a rational challenge to those who rely on common moral intuitions (or an inner sense of right and wrong) as a refutation of the happiness principle. Finally, Rachels closes with an important reservation about the merits of utilitarianism by introducing the idea of desert. A rational moral attitude needs to justify why someone has earned a certain amount of happiness, and utilitarianism does not seem equipped to offer this justification.

For appreciating the philosophical issues underlying utilitarianism, Rachels provides a clear account of the arguments. He is also helpful in addressing the idea of common sense as a reliable moral guide, especially when used by opponents of utilitarianism. Many virtue theorists support the idea of human flourishing, and Rachels's point that any rational moral philosopher needs to consider good consequences can be discussed later in the course when students are addressing specific virtues and vices.

Multiple-Choice Questions

1. A major difference between hedonism and the utilitarian view of happiness is that hedonism
   *a. considers something good because it brings pleasure.
   b. considers something pleasurable because it is good.

    c.   views physical pleasure as the only worthwhile good.
    d.   views intellectual, emotional, or spiritual goods as based on
         an illusion.

2.   For Rachels, the case of the Peeping Tom who takes pictures of a
     woman in her bedroom
     a.   indicates that utilitarianism is incapable of appreciating the
          right to privacy.
     b.   highlights the correctness of the hedonistic balancing of per-
          sonal pleasures and pains.
   *c.   supports the utilitarian case that Peeping Toms threaten the
          greatest happiness principle.
     d.   proves that moralists don't understand the secret delights of
          voyeurism.

3.   To those who rely on moral common sense, a utilitarian can
     respond that common sense
     a.   is not a Platonic form of the good.
     b.   often is not very common.
     c.   gets confused about long-term and short-term benefits.
   *d.   contains many irrational prejudices.

Discussion Questions

1.   Bentham says that "pleasures and pains are the *instruments*" a
     legislator has to work with; producing pleasure and avoiding
     pain are the goals of the legislator. If this is the foundation of
     utilitarianism, do you think Rachels is shifting the meaning of
     utilitarianism by distinguishing the good of pleasure from the
     good of happiness?

2.   Much of Rachels's discussion describes the weaknesses of moral
     common sense, often noted as the inner conscience, the little
     voice that tells you right from wrong, the gut feeling about good
     and bad. What are his main criticisms of common sense, and to
     what extent do you agree or disagree with him?

14. Immanuel Kant, "Good Will and Duty"

Although this too is a perennial favorite, it is a difficult read for most
introductory students. This is partly due to the density of Kant's writing. Moreover, the idea that duty rather than happiness forms the basis

of morality seems initially strange for most people. One way of introducing Kant's ethics is by highlighting his contributions in light of the moral debates of his own time. For example, J. B. Schneewind's recent book *The Invention of Autonomy* (1997) examines questions that moral thinkers were raising but not fully answering during Kant's time. Developing a theoretical response to these questions, Schneewind shows, ushers in Kant's idea of moral autonomy. Another way of illustrating Kant's major points is by emphasizing his attempt to capture common notions of fairness in a rational framework. As Nietzsche sardonically put it, Kant shows in language obscure to the commoner that the morality of the commoner is right. A third way to present his influence might portray current appeals to law as precedent-setting and universally applicable. The shortcoming of these approaches, of course, is that although they may help the student gain a sense of Kant's ideas, they hardly do justice to the depth of his thought.

As you likely have resolved your way of presenting the categorical imperative to introductory students, the only note to add is that the next selection by Bonnie Stelmach may help clarify in a livelier way the significance of Kant's moral ideas. How much attention you wish to devote to these ideas will determine whether you wish to cover both selections.

Multiple-Choice Questions

1. One's own happiness is important, but not in a moral sense, because people seek happiness out of
   a. rational goals rather than universal law.
   b. inclination rather than hedonic calculation.
   *c. inclination rather than duty.
   d. social utility rather than duty.

2. To make a promise with the intention of breaking it is immoral because it
   a. runs counter to the well-being of society.
   *b. is self-contradictory.
   c. contradicts the link between short- and long-term pleasure.
   d. conflicts with the Commandment on bearing false witness.

Discussion Questions

1. For many moral thinkers, one of the strengths of Kant's theory lies in its insistence that humans should never be treated solely as

a means. What do you think this principle means, and how practical do you think it is?

2. Kant argues that suicide is immoral. What are his reasons behind this position, and do you think it is consistent with his regard for moral autonomy?

15. Bonnie Stelmach, "A Dialogue between Generations for the 'Soul' Purpose of Understanding Immanuel Kant's Categorical Imperative"

For a more accessible presentation of the ideas related to the categorical imperative, Bonnie Stelmach recounts a dialogue between a grandfather, Phil, and his granddaughter, Sophy. She is worried about finishing a paper on Kant and winds up learning about her perspective by discussing it with her grandfather who studied philosophy in his younger days. Stelmach has them address the major points, including the relation of the categorical imperative to the golden rule, its application to the case of the inquiring murderer, whether a masochist should universalize his maxim, and its assumptions about human nature. The only part of the dialogue that gets technical is when Phil and Sophy distinguish the noumenal and the phenomenal self and their respective significance to Kant's moral ideas. Near the end of the dialogue Phil and Sophy reach a tentative agreement about a serious flaw in Kant's theory. What they see as Kant's awkward dualism between reason and emotion, freedom and inclination, generates an objection to the ability of a moral agent trying to universalize a maxim. This threatens his moral position with an absolutism that deprives it of any practical use.

To what extent you wish to explore Kant's ethics will determine how you use this dialogue. One option is to select passages from the dialogue and have students read them aloud, then go over the ideas with everyone. Stelmach's dialogue brings in related issues from Kant's other writings, and passages on the noumenal self or the causality of inclination may not be necessary to your plans for the course. Still, many discussions in virtue ethics debate the nature of the self that underscores the moral character. Stelmach's selection raises this issue from a different perspective, but one that might be worth addressing if the course begins to focus on the philosophical issues about the nature of the moral self.

Multiple-Choice Questions

1. Masochism, according to Sophy, could not be a universal moral law because
   a. there is no culture or society in the world in which masochistic conduct is legal.
   b. masochists confuse the golden rule with the golden ruler.
   *c. masochists act out of inclination rather than reason.
   d. by definition masochism violates the norms of natural law regarding self-preservation.

2. According to Sophy, Kant believes that in the case of the inquiring murderer, you should
   a. tell him only your name and Social Security number.
   b. reason with him about the evil of murder.
   c. offer a lie, but apologize after the anger has subsided.
   *d. tell the truth.

Discussion Questions

1. Why do Sophy and Phil suspect Kant flirts with a rather inhumane mentality? Clarify the reasons behind this suspicion and consider how Kant could be defended in light of other points raised by Sophy and Phil.

2. Central to their discussion is Kant's emphasis of reason over any other faculty because reason has a universal dimension that emotion, happiness, pleasure, and inclination lack. Further, they acknowledge that a rational ethics cannot resolve two worthy moral and universal principles. Can you devise your own example to highlight this issue? Do you think reason or nonrational faculties are best suited to reach a moral solution to your example?

16. Simone de Beauvoir, "The Ethics of Ambiguity"

In recent years there has been some question about the philosophical importance of Simone de Beauvoir. As an existentialist, she was generally placed under the umbrella of Sartre. As a feminist, her credentials have also been suspect. Some think her version of feminism is outdated; others are somewhat embarrassed by her seemingly subservient role in her relations with Sartre. And for many the importance of

27

existentialism as a philosophical and ethical attitude was played out a generation ago.

Yet much of the recent discussion of the "Other" is a serious attempt to engage or challenge the basic precepts of existentialist thinkers. Isn't, for Sartre, the failure to respond to the facticity of the subjectivity and freedom of the Other's presence a sign of bad faith? And though it gets caricatured in the media with epithets such as political correctness, New-Age spirituality, or the closing of the American mind, recent debates about the exclusion or assimilation of, say, immigrants, sexual deviants, or the poor, are often an extension of the fundamental existential respect for the freedom of how others choose to live. This respect for freedom is in part a response to other familiar moral theories introduced in previous selections, but this response seems most incisively formulated by Simone de Beauvoir.

Interweaving her thoughts on historical, literary, and philosophical thinkers, de Beauvoir captures what many college students of any generation worry about: Is there any one answer? By highlighting the meaning and value of ambiguity, de Beauvoir describes for the reader the uncertainty we experience when faced with a dramatic encounter. To the extent that the student as well as the teacher of ethics appreciates the meaning of such encounters, de Beauvoir makes a valuable contribution. In addition, this is one of the six or seven selections I rank as essential reading in the text, and some of the passages from this selection could be discussed in relation to any other part of the text.

Multiple-Choice Questions

1. For de Beauvoir, saving time and the conquest of leisure are meaningless unless you
   a. have projected worthwhile projects during your vacation.
   *b. are moved by the laughter of children playing.
   c. develop long-range plans to keep your membership with the local fitness club.
   d. can offer a rational articulation of a nonreligious morality.

2. In the conclusion, she says the ethics of existentialism is
   a. guided by Socrates' courage in facing his own death.
   *b. experienced by the truth of life.
   c. about the universal rights of free speech.
   d. rooted in the hedonistic sense of self.

Discussion Questions

1. Much of de Beauvoir's ethic centers on the value of freedom. From an existential viewpoint, do you think it is accurate to accuse the sociobiologist or genetic theorist of trying to avoid the importance of human freedom? Why, or why not?

2. Do you agree that an ethic of ambiguity can be of practical use? In light of de Beauvoir's account, how can this ethic help to judge moral conduct? Are there advantages or disadvantages to the existential approach when compared to, for example, Kant's or Bentham's approach?

17. Lao Tzu, "Wisdom and Artificial Codes"

This selection does not offer standard arguments, yet it is accessible to most students in terms of readability and raising questions. At the same time Lao Tzu is alert to the limitations of language to express the deepest of thoughts and truths. Neglect of these limitations often entices moral thinkers into all sorts of puzzles and paradoxes. One way of approaching these excerpts, then, is by focusing on Lao Tzu's discussion of nature or the Way. To the extent that people believe they have overcome the obstacles of nature, they likely have fooled themselves with their own artificial codes of right and wrong. This delusion is part human pride and part greed, thus setting the stage for the subsequent chapters on virtues and vices.

Another approach can focus on how Lao Tzu addresses ideas raised in earlier readings, particularly those on the nature of the self and the self's relation to the world. Because Lao Tzu does talk about the search for complete contentment, he invites comparisons with other thinkers who emphasize the importance of consequences in morality.

Multiple-Choice Questions

1. To reach complete contentment, Lao Tzu recommends that you
   a. make sure you graduate from college before you hate books.
   b. identify your highest ambition and then do everything to achieve it.
   c. pursue your ambitions but conceal them from others.
   *d. restrain your ambitions and avoid excess.

2. People develop artificial codes of right and wrong when they
   a. elect officials who do not carry out their campaign promises.
   b. reinterpret the moral lessons of sacred texts.
   *c. try to improve upon the normal functions of nature.
   d. feel the gods have ordained them to seek dominion over animals and nature.

3. To be much better off, intricate learning should be
   a. done in academic settings.
   b. pursued outside formal education.
   c. guided by a mentor who is also a moralist.
   *d. ignored.

Discussion Questions

1. Many moral philosophers believe nature is a poor guide for moral conduct. First, nature is not the world of harmony and tranquillity it sometimes appears to be; indeed, it can be quite harsh and cruel. Second, the appeal to nature overlooks the many benefits conferred to us in civilized life, such as medicine, art, technology, and travel, to name a few. How do you think a defender of Lao Tzu might respond to these objections? Is the same sense of nature being used? Develop your response in light of Lao Tzu's specific points and your view of nature.

2. Many of Lao Tzu's observations have to do with how human intelligence complicates and confuses rather than clarifies central features of moral conduct. Why does he say this? In light of other readings in the chapter, to what extent do you agree or disagree?

Chapter Review Questions

1. In the case study about two women tortured in South America, Lingis provides no comment after citing their report. From the readings in the chapter, which do you think help us make a moral judgment about torture? Though from the point of the victim no torture is acceptable, could someone use one of the readings to provide a moral justification of torture? Cite specific passages to support your response.

2. After reading the various theories about judging moral conduct, where do you stand on the possibility or importance of an objective basis in ethics? Select two or three readings to formulate your position.

3. Do you think the ideas of sociobiology or cultural relativism (as presented in Chapter 1) could provide an explanation of torture, such as the cruelty we inflict on one another is part of our genetic makeup or a way of ensuring the continuation of society's unity? Is it relevant that fervent religious believers have engaged in torture throughout history, often invoking the name of a god to defend their actions? Or do you think torture is ultimately inexplicable, an indicator of human madness? Clarify your thoughts about the meaning of torture and cruelty in human conduct.

Chapter 3
What Is Virtue Ethics?

Although a couple of earlier readings mention virtue, this chapter introduces virtues and vices as essential components in moral thought. It is also the shortest chapter in the book. For a graduate-level ethics course, philosophical attention to the theoretical aspects of virtue ethics is expected; many recent books and journal articles discuss the nature of moral character, the relation between virtue ethics and other traditional perspectives, or whether virtue ethics can displace utilitarianism, social justice, or deontology as the centerpiece of moral inquiry. For an introductory course, I thought it useful to keep a rein on the theoretical or metaethical analyses. Instead, many of the theoretical discussions appear in the context of discussing specific virtues and vices. The purpose of this chapter, then, is to highlight the perennial importance of virtue ethics.

The case study by Segal reflects on a touching and dramatic story about her grandparents in which the virtues of truthfulness and hope cannot both be respected. Hiriyanna outlines nine virtues as part of the Hindu approach to enlightenment and liberation. Jordan-Smith reviews the Western birth and life of the seven deadly sins. (In moral theology sin and vice are distinctive terms; here they will generally be used interchangeably.) Franklin recognizes thirteen virtues that encompass the search for moral improvement. For many moral philosophers, such as Alisdair MacIntyre, Aristotle is the anchor to systematic virtue ethics. In this first of three selections from Aristotle, virtue's relation to happiness, habit, and reason are addressed. The last selection comes from a recent essay by David Carr, who contends that virtue ethics is the basis for both a personal and a social/communitarian morality.

As described in this and the following chapters, a variety of candidates have been offered as virtue or vice. The so-called seven cardinal virtues are a combination of four pagan (temperance, justice, courage, and prudence) and three Christian (love, hope, and faith) virtues. The classic seven deadly sins include pride, anger, envy, lust, gluttony, greed, and sloth. The number seven has symbolic connotations, but it is safer to use it as a departure point rather than as a framework for presenting all the candidates for virtues and vices. In any event, you might keep in mind that many moral thinkers believed virtues and vices spanned the considerations in moral life. Even though its recent revival has been associated with conservative or personal issues, virtue ethics has through most of its history been viewed as significant for both individual and social morality.

Depending on the background of your students and how you want to organize presenting virtue ethics, the selections by Aristotle and Carr are fairly difficult and could be assigned after some discussion of specific virtues and vices.

18. Case Study: Lore Segal, "My Grandfather's Walking Stick, or The Pink Lie"

A popular way to introduce students to moral ideas is by illustrating a dilemma. Segal's case study presents two perennial virtues—hope and truthfulness—that appear to conflict in the story about her grandparents' experience in World War II. In clarifying her choice in choosing between hope and truthfulness, Segal spells out the rich meaning and value each virtue has. And last, her opting not to push the truth in light of her mother's retelling of the story is not intended to be a precedent-setting action. Rather, given the horror of the experiences of those who went through World War II, there are times when hope must be embraced at the cost of one's respect for truth.

Multiple-Choice Questions

1. To distinguish the pink lie from other kinds of lies, which aspect is NOT included?
   *a. sum of pleasures and pains for concerned parties
   b. intentionality of liar
   c. function of the lie
   d. moral reputation

2. In Primo Levi's reflection on the Nazi concentration camps and Jewish refugees, hope is
   a. an alternative to saving one's life by complying with the Nazis.
   b. the Christian way of triumphing over pagan evil.

*c. a way of rejecting an unendurable truth.
  d. strong evidence that good and evil will be dealt with in the afterlife.

Discussion Questions

1. Do you think there can be times when truthfulness and hope present a dilemma and the former should be supported? Devise your own example, either from experience or other readings, to show your understanding of the value of each.

2. Many people associate a hopeful person with starry-eyed optimism, someone who relishes in naivete or refuses to see the facts. How does Segal challenge this image while furnishing a deeper regard for hope? In light of the horror that shapes her case study, would you accept, reject, or revise her understanding of hope?

3. If hope is a virtue, is it something that everyone can have, or only some people? Clarify your answer.

19. M. Hiriyanna, "Philosophy of Values"

One advantage to this selection lies in its concise portrayal of a morality within a network of related truths and beliefs. The nine virtues highlighted by Hiriyanna are part of his overall view of how to understand the nature of the four values and their relation to the greatest goal, moksha. Toward the end of the reading, he addresses a rather technical distinction between dharma being an internal or external value. If your students are fairly strong in philosophical interests, then covering the entire essay is recommended. Hiriyanna's connections are thoughtful and systematic, deserving of close attention. However, if you are more focused on the moral aspects of Hindu thought, you might concentrate on the nine virtues listed by Hiriyanna. Discussion of, say, noninjury, cleanliness, or control of the senses will likely lead to Hiriyanna's other ideas and beliefs.

An additional caution here, and one that could easily apply to other selections, is that the role of ethics in other systems of thought could be a very difficult topic to cover fairly in an introductory course. As indicated by its etymology, universities have always brought together voices and ideas from different sources into a single forum. How we present these systems of thought may have great bearing on how their moralities are understood or misunderstood, whether they are subject to careful deliberation or hasty dismissal. The comforts of being virtuous persons due to our tolerance could be undermined by the inability to embrace one of Hiriyanna's virtues, sincerity.

Multiple-Choice Questions

1. Which is NOT included among the virtues?
   a. charity
   *b. justice
   c. love
   d. control of the senses

2. Yogi is important to the moral life because it
   a. allows one to overcome the concerns of personal experience.
   b. reflects the wisdom of the great Yankee sage, Y. Berra.
   *c. transforms intellectual belief into direct experience.
   d. allows one to gain the truth of oneself without paying for a therapist.

3. For Hiriyanna, the self-regarding virtues and the other-regarding virtues
   a. reflect the metaphysical dualism of the self.
   b. are logically incompatible.
   c. are linguistic tricks used by philosophers to confuse us about the true good.
   *d. are mutually related but distinct.

Discussion Questions

1. Which virtues listed by Hiriyanna do you find practical? That is, which ones seem to best represent you or your friends' approach to the moral life? If you think they are not useful virtues, are your reasons due to some other conception of the ultimate good? Explain your response.

2. Moksha is described as bliss and joy and, for many, the moment "when the self is released from bondage." Yet there is much dispute about the occurrence of this moment. Some contend that spiritual freedom is not attained until after physical death. Others think it possible to be enlightened and free. What are your thoughts about Hiriyanna's conclusion with its emphasis on the importance of the relation between physical death and moksha?

20. Paul Jordan-Smith, "Seven (and more) Deadly Sins"

This is another essential selection. Jordan-Smith articulates the historical background to the development of the sins or vices as a centerpiece of moral life. Though the number seven anchors this development, Jordan-Smith reminds the reader that many vices have been candidates as deadly sins. Moreover, he updates the discussion by reviewing how many current moral problems reflect the vices—but under different names. Isn't modern advertising an appeal to greed and vanity? Does the couch potato or computer nerd represent today's example of sloth? Are the worries about teenage pregnancy or sexual diseases another way of moralizing about lust? These are some of the questions Jordan-Smith raises.

A central part of this selection involves Christian theological thought on the meaning and hierarchy of the vices. The acronym "saligia" captures both the mnemonic device for learning the vices and the order of their deadliness. Succumbing to one vice, beginning with pride, leads to the harms brought about by other vices. Acedia, the earlier form of sloth, is the deadliest because it designates the death of the soul or spirit, for the individual has ceased to care about anything but his or her own physical needs. Not all religious thinkers adopted this ranking of the vices, of course, but Jordan-Smith's review highlights the intense thinking devoted not just to the single dangers of a vice but to the interrelation of the vices. Studying this interrelation involves moral attention to the self *and* concern for social good. The angry or envious person threatens his or her own well-being, and also endangers the well-being of others.

I have not edited any of Jordan-Smith's writing. However, his original essay did include many alarming illustrations of vicious demons in battle with virtuous agents over the souls of humans. The graphic depiction of the devil's warriors shooting arrows at aspiring virtuous persons, or the Virtues beheading Discord, invite comparison with current worries about violence and the media. I regretfully had to delete the illustrations, but I mention them for your own curiosity and as a way of dramatizing the historical and cultural significance of virtues and vices.

Multiple-Choice Questions

1. Which of the following phrases is NOT listed as an appeal to pride?
   a. "I'm worth it, because I believe in me."
   b. "Looking out for Number One."
   *c. "I have to love myself before I love others."
   d. "the me generation."

2. An example of sloth is the workaholic who
   a. always thinks of how to get ahead of coworkers.
   *b. engages in mindless industry and neglects spiritual goods.
   c. actually is a goldbricker when no one is looking.
   d. hoards money in order to get an early retirement.

3. Though pride heads the list of vices, it is, according to Aquinas, most escapable by engaging in
   a. solitary meditation.
   *b. humble action.
   c. rituals of self-denial.
   d. discussions with really successful people.

Discussion Questions

1. Do you think the vices are interrelated? If so, do you agree with the order of the "saligia," or would you revise the organization? If not, how do you think moral persons can overcome isolated vices?

2. How can you amend Jordan-Smith's observations of current vices? Which virtues does he or other essayists propose to be, in your opinion, the best opponents of current vices?

3. The vices are dangerous to both personal and social well-being contend many moral thinkers. Take one or two of the candidates for current vices and discuss whether their contention is accurate or mistaken. Give your reasons.

21. Benjamin Franklin, "Thirteen Virtues and Seeking Moral Perfection"

One of the recurring issues in morality—including virtue ethics—is whether and how people can improve. Is religious training essential? Are better laws or more stringent enforcement of them the key? Is early and continual moral education the answer? Franklin acknowledges the difficulty of reaching moral perfection. Still, the task is manageable if one takes it one virtue at a time. Interestingly, his proposal is largely an individual undertaking. Other than citing some venerable authorities, such as Cicero or Proverbs, Franklin's moral lessons involve careful reflection on one's daily activities. His emphasis on self-examination sounds like a variation of the Delphic Oracle's dictum to Socrates, "Know Thyself." How Franklin's schedule appeals to students and teachers concerned with ethics could spark discussion about the best methods of moral development.

Multiple-Choice Questions

1. The major obstacle to moral improvement is
   a. religious believers.
   *b. bad habits.
   c. ethics teachers.
   d. corrupt governments.

2. Silence is the second virtue to embrace because
   *a. one learns by listening rather than speaking.
   b. gossip is the worst social vice in Franklin's time.
   c. it is the best way to avoid telling lies.
   d. it is the second easiest virtue to perfect.

3. To avoid using words such as "certainly" or "undoubtedly" is Franklin's way of practicing
   a. deceit.
   *b. humility.
   c. temperance.
   d. frugality in speech.

Discussion Questions

1. Franklin seems to believe that once a virtue has been perfected, then another virtue can be worked on. His analogy with the gardener suggests that, once attended to, a virtuous habit is part

38

of one's moral character. Do you agree with this method of per-
fecting one's virtue at a time? Specify your reasons.

2. Why does Franklin write daily in a little book about his moral
    struggles? Can you think of a better way to examine thoroughly
    your own moral development, such as talking with a friend or a
    parent each evening, or getting on the Internet every night and
    sending out messages to an ethics chat room about one's moral
    improvement or downfall? Clarify your response.

22. Aristotle, "Virtue and Moral Character"

For many teachers of virtue ethics, Aristotle is the foundation for any
systematic view of the moral life. He combines reason, human nature,
happiness, and character in a way that supports the virtues as the anchor to the good life. You probably have taught this selection often
enough and made your own decisions on what to emphasize. I have
included here some additional material. Depending on how much of
Aristotle you want to cover or the background of your students, Chapters 1–4 on intellectual and moral attributes of character could be
omitted. Chapter 5 begins the more familiar discussion about virtues
and the means between extremes.

Multiple-Choice Questions

1. Virtues have to do with a person's
    a. passions.
    b. faculties.
    c. innate disposition.
    *d. character.

2. The extremes of confidence that underlie courage are
    a. pride and self-hatred.
    *b. rashness and cowardice.
    c. liberality and meanness.
    d. that one can never have too much fear.

3. The axiom "means between the extremes" for Aristotle is
    a. a principle that makes living a life of virtue a fairly easy
        compromise.
    b. a rational principle that involves mixing the right amount of
        excesses to reach a balance.

*c.   an indicator that it is not so easy to be good.
d.   a sign that some people are born moral and others immoral.

Discussion Questions

1.   When should moral habits begin, in Aristotle's view? Does his method for moral development compare favorably to Franklin's method? Be specific in your response.

2.   Can you apply the axiom "means between the extremes" to current examples? Select one or two examples discussed in the media or by your friends or classmates to determine whether Aristotle's approach is feasible. Keep in mind Aristotle's emphasis on reason, habits, and happiness.

23. David Carr, "The Primacy of Virtues in Ethical Theory: Part II"

Several recent journals and books have focused on the nature of the virtues. Some address the historical and psychological components of virtuous persons; others examine the relation of a life of virtue with other moral theories; others question the status of virtue theory as either independent of other theories or the core of the good life. Carr's contribution reviews these issues concisely. He first distinguishes the good of virtue ethics from the good in utilitarianism. The former emphasizes human flourishing, whereas the latter is mostly concerned with the production of more pleasure than pain. In addition, the good of virtue ethics is internal, in contrast to the external source of good that characterizes utilitarian values. Carr then addresses the possibility of identifying the right virtues. As seen just from the few selections so far, there is considerable discussion about the number and rank of the virtues or vices. He concludes by calling attention to the social or communitarian dimension of virtue ethics. In Carr's view many skeptics of virtue theory contend that it lacks a social ethic, at least one that goes beyond a specific cultural background. Carr's rejoinder claims that a core set of virtues seem universal, having moral value in nearly every society. The task for moral thinkers, then, is to reach some consensus, not so much about the status of virtue theory, but about the most important virtues.

As with Aristotle, Carr's selection could be presented before assigning the chapters on specific virtues and vices. Or, the issue about the personal/social dimension of virtue ethics and other moral theories might be raised after giving some attention to, say, anger and envy, truthfulness, or moral problems about ending a life.

Multiple-Choice Questions

1. The term "eudaemonia" is Greek for
    a. a happy or merciful death.
    b. the psychological obsession with physical appearance.
    *c. well-being as a rational and social endeavor.
    d. the happiness that all animals seek.

2. A teleological ethics is one based on
    *a. the good ends or results.
    b. democratic decision-making.
    c. long-distance communications.
    d. ancient myths.

3. By claiming that virtue ethics is part of the communitarian tradition, Carr means
    a. virtue ethics is a modern version of communism.
    b. morality must return to its religious roots.
    *c. the virtues draw from a cultural and social background.
    d. all of the above.

Discussion Questions

1. Carr contrasts virtue ethics with utilitarianism, even though both emphasize consequences. What are the key points that distinguish the two? Do you believe virtue ethics and utilitarianism agree or disagree about human nature? Be specific.

2. Bentham believes utilitarianism is primarily a social ethic. How is his version different from Carr's view of a communitarian ethic?

3. Near the end of his essay Carr asserts that the mainstream virtues are nearly universal, as are the vices. What does he mean by this? Do you agree or disagree with his view? Include your reasons with your response.

Chapter Review Questions

1. Which two or three virtues and vices introduced in the readings do you think are most important today? Which seem most outdated or irrelevant? Briefly explain your choices.

2. Assuming the virtues are worth developing, which thinker in this chapter offers the best approach for helping people become more virtuous or overcome the vices? Which one offers the least helpful approach? Spell out your reasons.

3. The case study by Lore Segal highlights a dilemma between truthfulness and hope. Which of the readings do you think proposes a moral solution to the dilemma? Critics of virtue ethics argue that moral dilemmas are best solved by an appeal to duty, law, or the greatest happiness principle, but *not* by an appeal to virtues. Developing virtues and avoiding vices may be good for encouraging moral character, the critics suggest, but resolving the nitty-gritty moral dilemmas that we often confront cannot be done within a virtue ethics perspective. Consider the solution you have proposed—does it answer the critics of virtue ethics?

Chapter 4

The Whole Truth and
Nothing But the Truth

Truthfulness is not one of the seven cardinal virtues, but virtue theorists do not treat truthfulness lightly. Indeed, without respect for truth the moral life seems either impossible or unworthy. To emphasize this respect, some recent moral thinkers have proposed truthfulness to be a virtue and deceit a vice. That is not to say that a moral person always tells the truth and never deceives. Rather, moral persons recognize the value in encouraging honesty and sincerity for one another as a basis for trust. Only by trusting one another can humans flourish as social creatures.

Skeptics of this view believe it is impractical and unrealistic. Humans have always needed a certain amount of deception. Without deception we could not get along. The moral issue involves the nature of the deception, its intentions and purposes. Moreover, everyday human life is such that we relish moments when the demands of worrying about or telling only the truth are suspended. Curiosity or gossip are such moments.

Most of the selections in this chapter address the value and meaning of being a truthful person. Doniger's case study reviews some historical and current stories of sexual deception. In addition to some of the amusing anecdotes, Doniger discusses whether men and women differ in terms of engaging this kind of deception. In the first of two contributions here, Bok explains the fundamental moral importance of truth telling; a lie, she argues, is rarely justifiable. Nyberg's rejoinder to Bok relies on everyday experiences where lying or deception are not only justifiable but even expected; many times we do not want to hear the truth. Mothersill begins her essay with the belief that truthfulness is a virtue, then cites recent public violations of this value. Closing her essay, however, she introduces a serious doubt regarding her moral stance. The dialogue by Smullyan is meant to be humorous with a purpose. The various speakers offer their views about why we tell the truth, with the "moralist" conducting the conversation at his own expense. The final two selections are more about a moral attitude toward knowledge than about truthfulness. Meilaender reviews the significance of curiosity, noting its positive and negative aspects. And Bok concludes the chapter with some insights about the nature and value of gossip, particularly in light of the tendency of mainstream philosophers to ridicule everyday conversation as idle chatter.

This chapter can be offered several ways. After the case study, the readings can be paired off. If you want to highlight a debate, Nyberg directly responds to the main points of Bok. Mothersill and Smullyan outline two perspectives on the complexity of truthfulness as a philosophical and moral issue. Meilaender on curiosity and Bok on gossip capture two aspects of knowledge that intrigue most anyone, including students.

Most of the readings are accessible enough to be part of student presentations. Students may use the ideas as departure points for their own studies about truthfulness and the importance of knowledge. The spirit of the essays also encourages students to reflect on their own respect for truth, whether telling it, hearing it, or seeking it.

24. Case Study: Wendy Doniger, "Sex, Lies, and Tall Tales"

Regardless of how much we profess to value the truth, in romantic and erotic moments truth is often the first casualty. Doniger's scholarly and witty investigation of sexual deception and masquerades suggests that people of all sorts avoid the truth. Although some of the masquerades seem incredible, Doniger's documentation of classic literary and current news sources gives evidence that in sexual matters humans willingly deceive others and themselves. She concludes with a court case in which the judge treats deception in human sexual conduct much differently than deception in other areas where fraud and harsh punishment would be the likely ruling.

Multiple-Choice Questions

1. By coining the phrase "veritas in coitu," Doniger means that
    a. people speak the truth after drinking some wine.
    b. there are significant truths in pornography.
    *c. there is truth in physical and spiritual elements of sexual love.
    d. deception works before having sex, but not after.

2. Though obviously not universal, a frequent difference between men and women in deception is that
   a. men's lies are mostly physical whereas women's are emotional.
   b. men act aggressively but want to be passive, whereas women appear passive but are not.
   *c. women's lies are mostly physical and men's lies are social and strategic.
   d. when women say "I love you" they are talking about an enduring emotion, whereas when men say "I love you" they are talking about a momentary interlude of pleasure.

3. According to Judge Posner, having sex by fraud is generally equivalent to
   a. a crime, just like fraud in taking money.
   b. a crime, just like rape.
   c. ordinary confusion of human communication.
   *d. seduction.

Discussion Questions

1. Doniger introduces a variety of examples to show how truthfulness and human sexual behavior are often contrary. From your experiences with recent movies, television shows, or readings in other courses, can you find examples to support or weaken Doniger's position?

2. Suppose you and your boyfriend or girlfriend read the Doniger essay and agree with her central points. Should either of you henceforth be upset if one catches the other in a lie? Why, or why not?

25. Sissela Bok, "On Truth-Telling"

This selection is somewhat detailed. It is composed of two passages from Bok's well-known book *On Lying*: the introduction and a sizeable part of the second chapter. How much you want to assign from this selection may depend on how thoroughly you plan on covering truthfulness. Some teachers believe that the issues on truthfulness are fundamental because they underscore a moral value that seems essential to social life—trust. Others feel truthfulness is important because it addresses a distinct feature of human nature—the importance of accurate and honest speech. And many think truthfulness should be an essential topic for an ethics course because it dramatically highlights the distinction between everyday practices (i.e., hedging the truth, withholding our real opinions, sugarcoating our views) and moral ideals (i.e., do not bear false witness, honesty is the best policy, tell it like it is). Bok addresses these issues in an accessible and informative manner.

The introduction to her book briefly reviews some commonplace occurrences of lying. She then notes that explaining the many cases of public deception and personal lying can be useful, but this does not take the place of contemplating and discussing the moral justifications to these cases. The section from her second chapter addresses the importance of trust and the hidden dangers of lying. A lie is rarely simple. Rather, it often leads to additional lying in order to conceal the original lie, and the lie harms not only the deceived person but the liar as well. She often cites government deception to illustrate her points. (In the conclusion to her book she proposes some directives for governments and institutions to follow in order to restore the public value for truthfulness. Social trust and personal integrity are at stake, she reminds us.)

I originally had planned to include Kant's rather infamous passage on the moral duty to tell the truth to a would-be murderer. Perhaps the inadvertent effect of Kant's view was that utilitarian considerations on happy results offered an easy alternative to Kant's apparent absolutism. One way of avoiding this rather simplistic dilemma is by first highlighting the value of knowledge and the importance of truth and deception in human life. Instead of emphasizing the justifications for lying, one can begin by discussing whether there is moral value in the courage to tell the truth. As far as we know, only humans worry about mustering the courage to tell the truth and nothing but the truth. Though Bok does not focus on courage and related virtues, her research and thinking on human truthfulness—and the responses to her thought—are one of the essential features of the text.

Multiple-Choice Questions

1. For those who regularly manipulate the truth and deceive others on the job, says Bok, one can look to
   a. prostitutes and other workers in the sex industry.
   b. rock 'n' roll singers with all their phony antics.
   *c. professionals such as lawyers and doctors.
   d. celebrities who claim that all they want is a normal life.

2. For Bok, trust is as much a social good as
   *a. the air we breathe and the water we drink.
   b. the electricity needed for computers and gasoline for our cars.
   c. having military and police departments to protect citizens.
   d. colleges requiring all students to take an ethics course.

3. According to Bok, the bias that blinds the liar can bring damage to
   a. other individuals and communities, but not the liar.
   b. the liar only after getting caught and punished.
   *c. everyone, including the liar.
   d. usually no one, since everyone engages in a little lying.

Discussion Questions

1. Bok contends that many liars have a "free rider" attitude, which means they believe they can lie to others but others should not lie to them. Do you think she has captured an insight about liars? How do you think Bok would respond to the "free rider" liar who says that he or she does not suffer from telling lies?

2. Are trust and telling the truth mutually dependent? That is, can one be trustworthy and deceitful, or can one tell the truth and not be trustworthy? What is Bok's and your response?

26. David Nyberg, "Truth Telling Is Morally Overrated"

If you like to present ethical problems in terms of a philosophical debate on morality in everyday life, the pairing of Bok and Nyberg might work very well. Nyberg's argument is based on his understanding of and challenges to Bok's arguments.

Briefly, Nyberg respects Bok's high regard for truth as a moral anchor. However, despite her many ordinary examples of lying, Nyberg believes that Bok is either unrealistic or too harsh about the value of everyday hedging of the truth. That most of us—regardless of gender, age, socioeconomic status, or rank of academic degree—engage in deception is not a sign of moral weakness. It indicates moral goodness. Emphasizing the virtue of prudence (practical wisdom), Nyberg argues that in many situations it is morally reasonable and beneficial to deceive or lie. Moreover, applying the golden rule, as Bok seems to do in her "free rider" point, cannot be a satisfactory counterargument. According to Nyberg, most of us not only deceive but often want to be deceived. In his words, "social life without deception to keep it going is a fantasy."

Again, how thoroughly you want to discuss truthfulness will determine whether to assign both Bok and Nyberg as entire selections or only portions. The section "Deception from the Bottom Up and Top Down" contains Nyberg's direct response to Bok. The decision may also be affected by the students, as the selections are somewhat long, though Bok and Nyberg are relatively free of technical or specialized writing.

Multiple-Choice Questions

1. "Humankind/Cannot bear very much reality" is a reminder from the pen of
    a. Lennon and McCartney, stars of The Beatles.
    b. Little Willie John, author of "Fever."
    c. Robert Frost, American poet.
    *d. T. S. Eliot, English poet.

2. The High IQ Half-Wit is someone who
    a. gets high grades but does not take moral philosophy seriously.
    *b. scores high on tests but is too arrogant to deceive on job interviews.
    c. does not get a job because he or she is only half as witty as the job interviewers.
    d. has excellent credentials on paper but in fact has no intellectual talent.

3. In response to Bok, Nyberg thinks that trust
    a. is irrelevant to the moral value of truthfulness.
    b. weakens whenever deception occurs.
    c. can only happen after people make general rules about deception and lying.
    *d. depends on deception to be sustained.

Discussion Questions

1. In contrasting Bok's "top down" approach and his "bottom up" approach, Nyberg criticizes philosophers' tendency to look for

48

abstract principles to resolve moral dilemmas. What do you think Nyberg's alternative to principles includes? Do you prefer his alternative? Why, or why not?

2. What is meant by "practical intelligence" (or prudence in virtue language)? What is the difference between practical intelligence and other kinds of intelligence?

3. Introducing each selection, Bok and Nyberg quote three epigraphs. Select at least one from Bok and one from Nyberg and show how they fit their respective essays. To what extent do they clarify an insight about the moral importance of truthfulness and deception?

27. Mary Mothersill, "Some Questions about Truthfulness and Lying"

For extended philosophical reflections on truthfulness, this selection by Mothersill and the next one by Smullyan provide worthy follow-ups. Mothersill begins with what seems to be a rhetorical question about truthfulness being a virtue. Surely it is, given how we teach children the value of truth and our understanding of the vice of hypocrisy. She illustrates some well-known cases of hypocrisy, from the Pentagon to journalist Joe Klein's dodge in confessing to be the anonymous author of *Primary Colors*. The moral outrage evoked by hypocrisy makes sense only if there is a shared and defensible moral belief in truthfulness.

She then outlines two major moral theories on truthfulness, consequentialism (or utilitarianism) and deontology (or Kantian ethics). In her view these theories have noticeable flaws (I have omitted some of her arguments). Yet her conclusion raises an important question for those who support virtue ethics. It seems, Mothersill observes, that truthfulness cannot stand as a virtue on its own. Being a truthful person has value only in relation to other virtues. What good is a truthful person who is also cowardly or intemperate? As some of the selections from Chapter 3 noted, a central concern in virtue ethics is not so much having sundry virtues but understanding the relation of the virtues to each other. On a note of self-examination, Mothersill concludes that she is not sure how to solve this problem, but she invites the reader to continue thinking about this fundamental moral topic.

Multiple-Choice Questions

1. During the 1991 Gulf War, the Pentagon's report that the Stealth fighter had 80% success was
   a. an understatement because military officials believe in the virtue of humility.
   b. accurate but unfairly reported by liberal-minded journalists.
   c. overstated because Congress wanted to reassure the public it wanted to win the war.
   *d. too high because, according to one reporter, the Pentagon was planning on getting more money from Congress.

2. Joe Klein is the
   a. public relations agent for the book *Primary Colors*.
   *b. author of the book *Primary Colors*.
   c. actor who portrayed President Clinton in the movie *Primary Colors*.
   d. actor who tried for the President Clinton role in the movie but was rejected because he couldn't pretend to enjoy Big Macs.

3. The answer to "Is truthfulness a virtue?" is, for Mothersill,
   a. clearly yes.
   b. no, since it is not part of the seven cardinal virtues.
   c. usually yes, if the consequences have greater pleasure for the greatest number.
   *d. uncertain.

Discussion Questions

1. Can truthfulness be a virtue on its own? Mothersill suggests no. What are her reasons, and do you agree or disagree with them?

2. How do you understand hypocrisy? Why is calling someone a hypocrite a moral judgment? Is being truthful at all times the best way to avoid becoming a hypocrite? Use passages from Mothersill's essay and your own observations or experiences to highlight your answer.

28. Raymond Smullyan, "Why Are You Truthful?"

Mothersill reviews some of the justifications or excuses made by those caught in a lie. The idea of understanding one's intentions in telling the truth is more widely reviewed by Smullyan in a witty and concise dialogue. With the Moralist serving as moderator, various individuals (the names proceed alphabetically) explain why they tell the truth. Each gives a reason, some echoing familiar ethical positions. (Some, such as the mystical hedonist, are coined by Smullyan.) Although the dialogue begins cordially, the participants, especially the Moralist, soon become testy. The Moralist no longer invites the participants to give their reason for truth telling—he wants them to give the good or right reasons, that is, persuasive and argumentative ones. Amid the exchanges Smullyan introduces several fine distinctions, such as the difference between subjective and objective reasons and the meaning of having a purpose. The dialogue is meant to honor Simplicus, and the conclusion deserves some attention when he is praised as the most truthful but confesses, "Me? Truthful? I had no idea that I was."

Multiple-Choice Questions

1. George tells the truth because he is
   a. a follower of the Ten Commandments.
   b. a mystical hedonist.
   c. a rational hedonist.
   *d. a selfish bastard.

2. According to Larry, the relation between "lower" and "earlier" is that
   *a. "lower" connotes inferior whereas "earlier" does not.
   b. "lower" refers to quality of life but "earlier" refers to quantity of life.
   c. they are equivalent in meaning.
   d. they are subjectively the same but objectively different in meaning.

3. In responding to the Moralist, Larry contends that one who says "I have no purpose in my doing X" and "There is no purpose in my doing X" is
   a. logically contradictory.
   b. simply insane.

c.   lacking human self-consciousness.

*d.   not much different from a tree.

Discussion Questions

1.   With which of the speakers do you most identify? least identify? Briefly explain your reasons.

2.   Of the readings you have covered in this chapter, which ones offer support to which participants in the dialogue? How does the moralist fare?

29. Gilbert Meilaender, "It Killed the Cat: The Vice of Curiosity"

The next two readings focus less on truth-telling and more on the value of knowledge and the ranking of truth. Should we be able to hear about anything we want? Are we entitled to study any aspect of life? Is there any constraint on the pursuit of knowledge that does not smack of censorship or oppression? These questions are pertinent in an academic setting, obviously. They also pertain to students' lives, whether as an issue of the First Amendment or recent disputes about the circulation of information through the Internet and other computer technologies.

Meilaender tries to reach a moral compromise between the extreme of careful regulation of knowledge and the unrestrained "anything goes" attitude. First he looks at the power of curiosity by reviewing a children's tale, *The Magician's Tale.* Though he recognizes that a child's and an adult's view of the tale may differ, Meilaender points out how curiosity in this and other children's tales is often a vice, but not always. The distinction lies in what the curious person wants to know and what he or she plans on doing with the knowledge sought. This introduces Meilaender's important distinction between useful and useless knowledge. The latter is morally significant when it involves the search for power and control. He then discusses Augustine, who considered curiosity a vice because it is linked with a lust of the eyes and can be more dangerous than the lust of the flesh (see Augustine in Chapter 6). This lust is illustrated by the desire to see a "mangled corpse." Apparently, "rubber necking" had its practitioners even in Augustine's time. One may also apply this "lust of the eyes" to local tragedies such as a fire or popular entertainment such as TV talk shows.

After discussing Augustine, Meilaender spells out the moral lesson and uncertainty in curiosity. The lesson partly involves the danger of seeking to know without any good or positive intentions, and how this danger harms others as well as the curious person through self-inflicted blindness. The uncertainty lies in how curiosity can be directed toward good rather than bad, and whether a person's own virtues can be the guide or whether some external source (e.g., God, law, social institutions, money) is required.

Multiple-Choice Questions

1. For Augustine, the "lust of the eyes" is exemplified when people get excited to see
   a.   visions of spiritual beings.
   b.   pornographic drawings or obscene writings.
   *c.   a mangled corpse.
   d.   the effects of a natural disaster.

2. To love the good and to have what we love are
   a.   the same.
   b.   compatible only for nonrational animals.
   *c.   not always compatible in this life.
   d.   compatible in the heat of erotic passion.

3. Which one is NOT a case of curiosity seeking to transgress the limits?
   a.   wanting to control rather than appreciating what is received
   b.   self-inflicted blindness
   c.   trying to know about the origins of the world without a vision of the One
   *d.   using technological instruments to explore the wonders of outer space

Discussion Questions

1. As a student, do you think there should be any limits on your intellectual curiosity? Why, or why not? Use examples to discuss your answer. In presenting your answer you might consider other forms of curiosity such as those having to do with national security or personal privacy.

2. How do you understand the title of Meilaender's selection? What is meant by the proverb "curiosity killed the cat" as

presented in his discussion of children's tales, by Augustine, or in the desire for possession?

30. Sissela Bok, "Gossip"

As Bok portrays gossip, it is more than a way of passing the time. Gossip is an important dimension of communication and everyday sociability. Hence its moral relevance is undeniable. To outline the moral aspects, Bok interweaves some passages from classic literature with observations of ordinary participation in gossip. In either form gossip is contrasted with more formal modes of communication, such as a business meeting, a college seminar, or a public lecture.

Bok defines gossip as having four components: informal, personal communication, about other persons, who are absent or excluded. She recognizes that often it is fairly harmless and is functional and productive at times. On the other hand, when gossip is malicious or false, it can have serious moral implications in its potential harm for other people. What she calls "reprehensible gossip" includes when someone: (a) reveals information that was promised to be kept secret; (b) conveys information that is knowingly false and intends to deceive the listener; or (c) is unduly invasive of someone's privacy.

Curiosity and gossip overlap in ordinary behavior. When meeting friends, chatting with colleagues, or phoning members of the family, people often want to know and like to tell the latest about other persons. To be someone's confidante in gossiping not only satisfies a bit of curiosity but also signals that you are respected as a moral person, one who will not abuse the trust with a vicious deed that Bok calls reprehensible gossip. If you want to make the moral value of truth one of the central features of your course, this essay may be an eye-opener for students, particularly in its conclusion wherein Bok questions the traditional philosophical dismissal of everyday conversation.

Multiple-Choice Questions

1. Which category is NOT part of reprehensible gossip?
   a. breaking another's confidence
   b. information known to be false
   *c. not applying the golden rule
   d. clearly invading another's privacy

2. Many people engage in gossip, so for someone to be known as a gossip means the person is
   a. probably most trustworthy.
   *b. probably suspicious.
   c. bored with life.
   d. the life of the party.

3. When well-known philosophers such as Kierkegaard or Heidegger rail against everyday conversation, they
   *a. show their own misunderstanding of the depths of human communication.
   b. prove why philosophers are considered the most insightful seekers of wisdom.
   c. forget that they too participate in trivial or idle chatter.
   d. remind us that all of us are hypocrites.

Discussion Questions

1. What are the four components of gossip, as defined by Bok? If you agree with the definition, does she help us understand why gossip is not allowed in the classroom, or some other formal setting? If you disagree with her definition, specify the changes you would make and why.

2. How do you distinguish a good from a bad gossip? Have you ever told another person some information that you later regretted sharing? Has someone ever regretted telling you information because you violated one of the three categories of reprehensible gossip? In either case, is reprehensible gossip a sign of a momentary mistake or bad moral character? Explain your answer.

Chapter 5
Struggling with Anger, Envy, and the Virtues

This chapter deals with two of the classic vices. As earlier readings (e.g., Jordan-Smith, Carr) indicate, anger and envy are powerful forces because they threaten harm to others, society, and the self. They also continually draw the attention of moral thinkers because anger and envy seem peculiar to human nature. True, animals get enraged, but only humans seem capable of contemplating and inflicting intense pain on others as a way of satisfying their anger. On the other hand, many moralists believe anger can be righteous within certain contexts. Envy has its own troubles. It is less direct than anger. By outward appearances an envious person seems comfortable and successful. Inwardly, however, an envious person is never satisfied because that person only sees what others have and begrudges their well-being, regardless of the person's own accomplishments or good fortune.

Are all of us given to fits of anger or temptations of envy? If so, why do some manage to constrain these vices whereas others virtually become slaves to them? Are these issues strictly personal, or are there social and cultural forces that foster anger and envy? Which virtues might be nurtured so that a moral person can overcome anger and envy? Are there social influences that contribute to our struggles against the dangers of anger and envy?

The selections in this chapter address these questions by focusing on how anger and envy affect both personal and social morality. Moreover, some raise candidates of virtue capable of triumphing over these deadly vices. The case study by Burrows concisely illustrates the power of angry mobs bent on gaining vengeance. A vigilante group, notes the historian, comprises a force greater than the sum of its individual parts. That is, individuals who are mostly cowards suddenly gain a new boldness or courage when they behave like a herd of beasts, a crazed mob, or a drunken crowd.

56

This insightful study is followed by discussions about the nature and moral status of anger. Auden links excessive anger to a kind of pride, for only a vain or selfish person could take his or her own suffering as the most important evil in the universe. Aquinas distinguishes several kinds of anger that get expressed through the desire for revenge. Most are vicious. Only in relation to divine anger could something so horrible as capital execution be considered just. A more introspective focus on anger is beautifully described in Gordon's depiction of the transformation one undergoes in the midst of *being* angry.

One of the classic virtues is justice. As William Casey (*Pagan Virtues*) describes it, justice was one of the four essential virtues of pre-Christian and Christian thought. There are many important debates about justice; here justice is discussed as one response to the dangers of anger. One of these debates concerns the death penalty, which has increased both in popular support and actual practice during the last decade. Greenberg argues that the American, and maybe any country's, use of the death penalty is morally flawed. The legal execution of criminals is invariably unfair—and if unfair, necessarily unjust. Van den Haag's rejoinder to this position emphasizes the value of the proper expression of anger. Vengeance is sometimes distorted by its opponents. In fact, he claims, vengeance properly done is an essential component of a good society.

Another candidate for a virtue to battle anger appears in Seneca's idea of clemency. Is forgiveness a sign of foolishness or weakness? No, argues Seneca. But for people to see the value of clemency as the most important virtue it needs to be embraced by the ruler of the people, and then by family members, friends, and anyone who wants to be a good person. So clemency is a sign of wisdom and strength.

Envy as a different kind of problem for justice is raised by Rawls. To the extent that envy is a well-known attribute of human beings, those striving for a just society need to pay attention to envy. Sometimes envy can be a symptom of an unjust society. Other times, unfortunately, envy can be the cause of injustice. How to prevent this latter form of envy is part of Rawls's argument for the equal distribution of some—but not all—essential goods. The selections by Nietzsche highlight a negative and a positive view. His discussion of *Schadenfreude* (the German term referring to the pleasure or joy we receive when seeing or hearing of another's misfortune or sorrow) casts a dim view of human beings. The second selection has Zarathustra proclaiming a bestowing virtue, one that seems to delight in giving, a strength that reminds one of a god, the sun, or a possible form of human existence.

How to assign selections of this chapter probably depends on the relation between what you want them to at least know and what you think they would like to study and discuss. Capital punishment is a perennial favorite. Sometimes its familiarity harms rather than helps thoughtful discussion. Still, Greenberg and van den Haag offer insightful observations about justice and the proper expression of anger. The case study on vigilantism could be a lead-in to this discussion. On the other hand, many students might want first to discuss the nature of anger. They, too, have experienced anger in some of its various forms. They have been angry and been subject to the anger of others. Reading Auden and Gordon could then be a way to follow up the case study. The style of these two selections, by the way, is elegant and concise so they could be assigned at the same time.

If you want to address envy but are pressed for time, you might assign just the beginning of Rawls and a couple of the more direct selections by Nietzsche. However, if your tendency in teaching introductory ethics is to emphasize some general disputes about human nature or cultural problems, the contributions of Rawls and Nietzsche are essential, even in these brief excerpts.

Another way of approaching the recurring importance of the struggles between the virtues and vices is historical. This approach can appreciate today's problems while reminding us of how they have been recurring throughout the ages. Aquinas's argument on the possible justice in capital punishment and Seneca's praise of clemency as the primary virtue of a king and his people reflect two concise perspectives on the struggle between virtues and vices.

31. Case Study: William E. Burrows, "Vigilante!"

In this brief excerpt from his study of the historical and contemporary aspects of American vigilantes, Burrows illustrates the dynamics of vigilante mentality. He also hypothesizes about the five salient features of vigilantism. Since this was written in the late 1970s, it might be worth asking students to see if his hypothesis has worked out. In any case, Burrows clearly presents the temptations to and dangers of vigilante conduct.

Multiple-Choice Questions

1. The performance artist who invited an audience to slice up her dress with scissors was
   a. Mae West.
   *b. Yoko Ono.
   c. Madonna.
   d. Boy George.

2. In Albany, New York, what was NOT said by the crowd to a man considering a suicide leap?
   a. You're yellow.
   b. Jump! Jump! Jump!
   *c. Wait! The TV cameras aren't here yet!
   d. C'mon, you're chicken.

3. The fifth feature of vigilantism is that vigilante committees form when the upper segment of society feels
   a. that communism is making a revival in other countries.
   b. threatened by an influx of illegal immigrants.
   c. angry that season tickets to the NFL games are no longer tax-deductible.
   *d. threatened by those socially or economically inferior to them.

Discussion Questions

1. What is Burrows's view of mob behavior? Do you agree?

2. Does Burrows overlook the power of crowds to use righteous anger? That is, is it possible for a group of people to be virtuous rather than vicious? Are there certain features or conditions needed for this possibility? How do they compare to the features outlined by Burrows on the emergence of vigilantism?

32. W. H. Auden, "Anger"

There are two kinds of anger, according to Auden. Natural anger, exhibited by all animals, is a reflex rather than a voluntary action. When anger is chosen, it then enters the moral realm. Anger can be functional, such as the coach chewing out his players, or it can be trivial, such as cursing under your breath when caught in traffic.

59

Usually anger is sin, a manifestation of pride insofar as the angry person believes that his or her existence is more important than anyone else's.

In his delineation of kinds of anger, Auden questions those who think their anger accomplishes any good and those who believe in the wrath of God as a form of justice. His conclusion focuses on the possibility of Hell as the ultimate expression of righteous anger. For Auden, the idea of eternal torture makes little sense and does not speak well of a merciful deity. If there is a Hell to the sin of anger, he notes, it springs not from God's wrath but from the angry person's own insistence on clinging to his own distorted sense of self-importance and not facing reality.

Multiple-Choice Questions

1. In contrast to natural anger, humans are capable of the sin of anger because they have
    a. the capacity of foresight and symbolization.
    b. court systems and prisons, unlike animals.
    c. the faculty for memory and torture.
    *d. the faculty for symbolization and memory.

2. According to Auden, the belief that retribution is a just expression of anger
    *a. rests on a fallacy.
    b. is the only rational and acceptable expression of human anger.
    c. makes sense only if one accepts religious morality.
    d. best explains the revival of capital punishment.

3. Many people enjoy anger so much that when the object of their hate is destroyed they
    a. go to the funeral and cheer.
    b. wear black clothes for six months.
    *c. fall to pieces because hatred was their reason for living.
    d. buy a dartboard posted with a picture of the object of their hate.

Discussion Questions

1. Auden rebukes Christians who believe Hell awaits sinners. Summarize his key points about God and Hell. Do you agree or disagree with his points? Explain.

2. Anger as a sin is either futile or unnecessary, says Auden. If he is right, how can he explain why anger seems to be so prevalent, from an increase in criminal punishment to shootings by teenagers? Is there rationality to anger not recognized by Auden?

33. St. Thomas Aquinas, "On Vengeance"

Vengeance and anger often go hand in hand. Does that make vengeance a vice? Not completely, argues Aquinas. There are times when vengeance can be a virtue, and exacting punishment for wrong-doing is lawful and rational if done in the context of divine rather than personal anger. One who exacts vengeance, writes Aquinas, "simply exercises a God-given power." Moreover, he points out that punishment is not contrary to but part of the law of love. Vengeance on a group of people can also be morally permissible, but more often the sins of a community should be met by punishing either the community's principal leaders or its most influential faction.

Other virtues and vices associated with vengeance include courage, charity, cruelty, and unwarranted mercy (illustrated in the maxim "spare the rod and spoil the child"). Aquinas, in the Third Point, supports capital punishment: first, it can have medicinal purposes for the sinner; second, some punishments can terrify more than the sin can attract a potential sinner. The selection here is, of course, little more than a snippet from Aquinas's voluminous writings on virtues and vices. Whether you want to emphasize the theological anchor to his thought or highlight his understanding of the morality of vengeance as a contribution to current problems partly depends on your approach to this chapter.

Multiple-Choice Questions

1. Vengeance can be lawful if the avenger's intentions
   a. are to cleanse himself of his own anger.
   b. meet public approval.
   c. avoid vigilante actions and seek the help of police.
   *d. are aimed at the good, such as correcting the wrongdoer.

2. The two vices against vengeance are
   a. sloth (too lazy to punish) and pride (distorting one's own suffering).
   *b. cruelty (too much punishment) and neglect (not punishing at all).

c. lust (getting pleasure from punishing) and gluttony (enjoying a meal while punishing).

d. cruelty and pride.

Discussion Questions

1. Can a Christian, or any religious person, support divine love and divine wrath in which someone is sentenced to eternal suffering? Auden and Aquinas are opposed here. How does Aquinas defend his position? Develop your response to his main points on this issue.

2. Can vengeance be a personal virtue without being a social or divine virtue? Or is vengeance primarily a social or divine virtue, and only secondarily a personal virtue? Cite passages from Aquinas to clarify the ranking of types of vengeance.

34. Mary Gordon, "Anger"

Auden and Aquinas disagree about the religious attitude toward anger. But have they understood the complex nature of anger? One account of the enduring power of anger lies not in the human faculty for memory or justice but in the sheer joy that anger brings to most people. As with other intense experiences, such as love or insight, anger can be transforming. In being angry a person is often not the same person. In this transformation, however long it lasts, one's relation to other people and to the world also changes.

These points are elaborated and richly described by Gordon. Although moral philosophers prefer arguing the justifications to different forms of vengeance, Gordon tends to undercut their positions by showing how anger often has a life of its own. She supports this with reflections on classic writers such as Dostoyevsky and personal anecdotes such as her own fit of anger witnessed by family members. Is there a human power sufficient to overcome the joy and the danger of anger? In the conclusion Gordon invokes the moment of forgiveness, in its silence and emptiness, as the only irrational deed strong enough to battle the irrational force of anger. As a conventional philosophical presentation of moral issues, this essay might be omitted. As a philosophical inquiry about being human, I recommend Gordon's essay as one of this text's nine or ten chosen for the beauty of the writing, wit, and insight.

Multiple-Choice Questions

1. The center and source of anger is
    a. the brain, for it remembers the cause of one's suffering.
    *b. the mouth, since it relishes tasting and talking about anger.
    c. the heart, because it is the seat of the passions.
    d. the stomach, given how people hunger for vengeance and can hate another's guts.

2. Gordon experienced the temporary transformation induced by anger when she had a fit and
    a. threw and broke some of her mother's favorite chinaware.
    b. took an ax to the television set because her children refused to enjoy the nice weather.
    *c. pounded on the family car because no one would help her in the kitchen.
    d. ran a lawn mower through the neighbor's garden because of their noisy dog.

3. The best antidote to being angry at another person is, in Gordon's words,
    a. proper rather than excessive vengeance.
    *b. irrational forgiveness.
    c. rational dialogue with the target of one's anger.
    d. to hire a damn good lawyer.

Discussion Questions

1. Why does Gordon think there is much joy in the experience of anger? Briefly explain her reasons, giving some attention to what she means by "joy."

2. Do you agree that feeling and expressing anger can be transforming? Gordon describes how many people almost become animal-like in their fits of rage and anger. Have you observed or experienced such a transformation? Do you think Gordon's proposal to overcome anger is moral or practical? Why, or why not?

35. Jack Greenberg, "Against the American System of Capital Punishment"

This issue you no doubt are familiar with. Along with abortion and assisted suicide (see Chapter 9), capital punishment has been a staple for many introductory ethics courses. Although there is always the danger that students may be numbed by the frequent public discussion of these issues, in my opinion students have not had much of a chance to study these issues in an intellectually stimulating climate. As ethics instructors, we can provide that climate. In the case of capital punishment, there is the added drama of debating whether some monster featured on the evening news deserves to live after gunning down three innocent citizens.

I have included two fairly recent essays that present contrary positions on capital punishment. Both emphasize the value of justice. Whether you want to present both Greenberg and van den Haag as a debate, or situate them in the context of personal and social expressions of vengeance as discussed by earlier selections, largely depends on how much attention you or your students wish to give to this topic.

Greenberg presents his case carefully and concisely. He recognizes the frustration many citizens express when talking about the futility of inadequate punishment for horrible crimes. The worst case scenarios, however, do not represent the nature of the American practice of capital punishment. Citing the 1979 execution of John Spenkelink as a departure point, Greenberg argues that the erratic and arbitrary use of capital punishment is inherent in the American criminal justice system and hence contrary to the Constitution and unjust. To other arguments for capital punishment, Greenberg points out that executions do not deter potential criminals or murderers, the racial and economic bias of capital punishment is undeniable, and life imprisonment is the maximum form of punishment we should use.

Multiple-Choice Questions

1. In the United States the racial bias of capital punishment is directed against
   a. whites.
   *b. blacks.
   c. illegal immigrants.
   d. first-generation immigrants.

2. Other nations in the Western democratic world that have legalized capital punishment include
   a. Great Britain and Germany, but only for political terrorists.
   b. Spain, France, and Italy, as a response to local anarchists.
   c. Germany and Italy, as a leftover from their fascist past.
   *d. none.

3. Greenberg thinks capital punishment is not a general deterrent
   because most killers
   a. are too clever to get caught.
   b. get lawyers who know the tricks of the court system.
   *c. act impulsively.
   d. do not know the laws about first-degree and second-degree
      homicide.

Discussion Questions

1. If the United States could correct the racial bias in its use of capital punishment, would Greenberg then support it? Which passages in his essay support your answer?

2. Why does Greenberg think executions constitute "cruel and
   unusual punishment," which is forbidden under the Constitution? Do you agree or disagree with his view? Explain.

36. Ernest van den Haag, "The Ultimate Punishment: A Defense"

The idea of justice encompasses many aspects of social and personal
morality. What the Greeks or Christians meant by justice in placing it
among the top virtues is subject to many scholarly discussions. By
including it here we want students to gain at least some sense of the
importance of justice with regard to a particular issue. The contribution by van den Haag emphasizes the value of justice by saying that if
capital punishment is morally wrong then it is wrong regardless of its
erratic or racially biased application. If capital punishment is morally
permissible, however, then the charges of injustice by abolitionists are
misdirected. Correct the unjust uses, but do not condemn the morality
of capital punishment.

65

In any case, van den Haag questions whether there is in fact racial discrimination in the criminal justice system. His response to the "mistaken conviction" objection is that mistakes that cost human life occur everywhere; we do not stop all construction, he notes, because some workers die from accidents on the job. He recognizes that the deterrence theory is difficult to verify with any systematic and consistent data. Yet that is not so important, for retribution—the just expression of the evil of the crime—is van den Haag's central argument for defending capital punishment. The idea that executions are cruel, uncivilized, or degrading is not supported by some famous philosophers such as Kant or Hegel. Nor does it reflect the beliefs of ordinary citizens. In fact, the murderer, not the government or its vengeful citizens, has already dehumanized himself, says van den Haag. In such a state, execution is the only fitting response.

Multiple-Choice Questions

1. In refuting the racial bias of capital punishment, van den Haag claims that
   *a. criminal guilt is based on persons, not groups.
   b. some traditional minorities have engaged in clever public relations campaigns.
   c. racial bias is actually less of a problem than the bias against all males.
   d. economic bias is the real culprit, for it causes racial bias.

2. To those who protest that capital punishment legitimizes killing, van den Haag answers that
   a. no other democratic country worries about this.
   *b. imprisonment is not thought to legitimize kidnapping.
   c. we should consider televising executions.
   d. legitimacy is irrelevant for cases of anger and vengeance.

Discussion Questions

1. One point of contention between death penalty disputants concerns the value of dignity (or humanity). What do the disputants mean by dignity or humanity in punishment? In your view, is capital punishment a sign of indignity or inhumanity or an act of dignity or humanity? Explain.

2. Van den Haag disagrees with the abolitionist argument that the rare possibility of executing an innocent person makes capital punishment immoral or illegal. His analogy is that accidental deaths occur in all activities of life, but we do not stop these activities. Is this a fair analogy? Be specific in your response.

37. Seneca, "On Clemency"

That anger can easily turn into cruelty is hardly a recent discovery. As Seneca acutely notes to the Roman tyrant Nero, cruelty is more than anecdotal—it can corrupt a society. Humans by nature are not cruel. But they can become cruel if anger and vengeance are not controlled. The source of this control, according to Seneca, begins at the top, with the emperor or the prince of the people. (In fact, it actually begins with the gods and how we want them to treat us.) Hence, the political leader is also a moral exemplar. No doubt this invites comparisons with recent political leaders in both democratic and non-democratic arenas. For Seneca, however, the leader should do more than control the urge to punish severely. The leader should practice clemency, the virtue "most becoming to a human." For clemency (or mercy), the power to forgive humans their moral flaws and occasional vicious deeds, is the virtue most capable of preventing the outbreak of cruelty. In that sense, clemency is in Seneca's view an essential personal and social virtue.

This selection might be broken up, depending on how thoroughly you plan on covering this chapter. If you want to emphasize the significance Seneca attaches to clemency and cruelty, sections 2, 3, 4, 5, 25, and 26 should suffice. I included the middle section for those who are also interested in Seneca's thoughts on the gods and issues of his own time. However you treat the essay, the human capacity for clemency or mercy is an enduring issue in moral thought.

Multiple-Choice Questions

1. Clemency is becoming for humans, but most becoming for
   a. religious leaders.
   *b. political leaders.
   c. moral saints.
   d. all those angry guests on television talk shows.

2. For Seneca the vice of cruelty is
   a. inborn in all humans.
   b. mostly practiced in nonreligious societies.
   *c. not innate to humans.
   d. a personal rather than a social danger.

Discussion Questions

1. Seneca observes that "mercy will make whatever house she enters happy." What do you think he means by mercy (or clemency)? How can one embrace or practice it? Should you forgive those who have harmed you? Why, or why not?

2. What do you think Seneca would say to those debating the morality of capital punishment? Do you think his view of clemency is a worthy alternative? Explain your reasons.

38. John Rawls, "The Problem of Envy"

For many moral thinkers, envy is one of the most insidious vices. Envy disguises itself, cloaking itself in positive terms while it actually seeks to demean or deprive others of their accomplishments or well-being. In that sense envy is as much a social as a personal vice. This might explain why Rawls, who gives little attention to virtues and vices in *A Theory of Justice,* devotes a couple of sections to the relation between envy and social justice. On one hand, envy can be a symptom of inequality; citizens begrudge what others have because the distribution of social goods is unfair. On the other hand, envy can be a cause of unfairness. People are not content with their own accomplishments because their primary worry is what others have. The second kind of envy concerns Rawls because it threatens to undermine any efforts in developing a society based on his two fundamental principles of justice.

Presenting Rawls to introductory students may require some background, such as the central themes of his book or the importance of his two principles. Pointing out the value of basic equalities, the "difference" principle, opportunity, confidence, and self-esteem might help students appreciate the danger of envy in Rawls's moral outlook. Again, given how envy is not easily identifiable, you might ask students about examples of envy in their own lives, whether in school, at work, or where they live. If you want to highlight envy without getting too involved in Rawls, you might assign just the first part of the selection where the psychology of envy is outlined.

Multiple-Choice Questions

1. An envious person is willing to
   a. deprive others of their goods if those goods go to the envious person.
   b. allot benefits to others only if more benefits go to the envious person.
   *c. deprive others even if the envious person must lose something good.
   d. allot goods to others only if the goods have no monetary value.

2. For Rawls envy is excusable or rational when it is a reaction by a person who
   *a. loses self-respect.
   b. suffers a history of jealousy syndrome.
   c. has had a lot fewer lucky breaks than the rest of us.
   d. is by nature competitive.

Discussion Questions

1. Why does Rawls say that envy is a personal and social vice? From your own observations or experiences, can you offer an example of envy that supports Rawls's view, or an example of envy that has positive rather than negative effects?

2. How are spite, jealousy, and envy related to one another? How are they distinct? Do you think they are attributes that most people have, at least to some degree? Does Rawls offer a solution that can best counter the dangers of envy?

39. Friedrich Nietzsche, *"Schadenfreude and Envy"* and "Of the Bestowing Virtue"

How to present Nietzsche to introductory students can be tricky. He is probably one of the few philosophers they have heard about, and what they have heard is usually about the death of God, the Superman, or his madness. A first reading of him can also be tricky, since he uses little philosophical jargon. Although his reputation for writing in an aphoristic style is somewhat misleading (the sections often have a continuity), it is worth keeping in mind that Nietzsche himself likened his writing to throwing lightening bolts. To be a recipient of a couple of these bolts should be one of the experiences of college life. Hence I think this is one of the essential selections in the anthology.

Many think of Nietzsche as a moral nihilist. The first selection on *Schadenfreude* (the German term meaning a delight one feels in the suffering of others) and envy shows why. Envy is portrayed as the kind of feeling that gives many humans a purpose for living. So important are envy's cousins—punishment, cruelty, and revenge—that the idea of equality and justice appear either useless or disruptive to the vicious pleasures most humans enjoy. That Nietzsche seems to delight in this analysis is one reason he is viewed as a nihilist.

Others see Nietzsche as offering a positive morality. To give students some evidence for this, I have included Zarathustra's praise of the bestowing virtue. It highlights a different way of looking at the selfish attributes by emphasizing the power to give. This power may be another candidate in helping humans with their struggle against the dangers of anger or envy.

Multiple-Choice Questions

1. According to Nietzsche, malicious joy or *Schadenfreude* has only existed since the
   a. emergence of capitalism.
   b. dawn of official religion.
   *c. foundation of society.
   d. moment Adam was ashamed in front of Eve.

2. In the section titled "Elements of Revenge," which is NOT an exception to the principle that everyone avenges himself?
   a. having no honor
   b. loving the offender
   *c. seeking an apology from the offender
   d. being inspired by contempt

3. Talking with his disciples about the bestowing virtue, Zarathustra says the phrase "All for me" is
   a. the future of Western morality.

*b. a horror to us.
c. the real principle of justice.
d. how rich people think.

Discussion Questions

1. Nietzsche's account of envy and *Schadenfreude* includes an idea of punishment that has more to do with restoring honor and gaining pleasure by inflicting harm. Can you think of recent social and cultural trends or personal experiences that support or weaken Nietzsche's account? For example, the prison population in America has doubled over the last ten to fifteen years. How does Nietzsche's analysis help us understand this phenomenon? You might devise your own example.

2. How does the "bestowing virtue" reflect an understanding of selfishness? Is it similar to or different from other views of selfishness you have read? Is the bestowing virtue possible or practical?

3. In the section titled "The Virtues That Damage Us," Nietzsche contends that virtues such as justice are society's invention to force equality on individuals who are unequal. Superior individuals embrace pride rather than justice. Do you see this as a case of moral nihilism or a negative ethic? Why, or why not?

Chapter Review Questions

1. In your view, what is the significance of anger or envy? Do you think most human beings are subject at one time or another to them? Can they be productive as well as destructive? If you think anger or envy can be productive, offer a brief explanation of how they should be encouraged. If they are destructive, which of the virtues introduced in the chapter do you think is best or least equipped to help moral persons win the struggle against anger or envy?

2. Many of the discussions in this chapter address human nature insofar as they try to understand what happens to people when they experience anger or envy. Which of the readings do you think offers the most accurate and least accurate portrayal of

what happens to people when anger or envy guide their conduct? Develop your answer, citing passages from the readings you selected.

3. Imagine you could invite several of the writers in this chapter to appear in a symposium at your college to discuss one another's ideas. Which ones would you invite, and why? What topics would you want them to address, and what questions would you ask them?

Chapter 6
Is It All You Need?
Variations on the Love Ethic

The themes in this chapter are familiar to nearly everyone. Yet while students may be in, dream about, reflect on, or desire love, discussing love in a philosophical way is often as difficult as experiencing it. With that in mind I have included selections that tend to address love in one of three ways. The first involves different notions of love. The second way discusses love in relation to other virtues and vices. The third focuses on some of the personal and social dimensions of love. Obviously, these three ways can overlap. Some examples: Theano addresses the relation of marital love, jealousy, and the husband's lust; Nyberg reviews the relation between prudence, trust, and the love between friends; Vatsyayana talks about love, loyalty, and obedience. Rather than use the classic delineation of love as eros, agape, and philia, I have used lust, friendship, marital, and familial love as the categories for organizing the selections in this chapter. (Additional discussions on love as concern for the other can be found in Chapter 8: see Plato, Hildegard von Bingen, Daniel Berrigan, writers on the care virtue, and Royce.) Hence the selections can be used as part of a systematic effort in studying love or assigned piecemeal according to topics that interest you or your students.

The case study by Mairs is witty and self-deprecating, but intense. After reading "On Not Liking Sex," several female students have remarked that every man should read it. Augustine offers one of the classic Christian statements on the dangers of sexual desire; it might be worth noting how Augustine's analysis emphasizes that the power of lust is so great that it, unlike any other vice, escapes self-control. The selection from the Kama Sutra advises how a loyal wife should treat her husband in a subservient way. The follow-up by de Beauvoir examines more thoroughly the complex relations between a man in love and a woman in love. If you are interested in discussing sexual relations as part of a larger network of power relations, the case study by Mairs prepares the student for reading Vatsyayana and de Beauvoir together.

Most students are familiar—perhaps more than their teachers—with the emergence of cyberspace, the Internet, chat rooms, or what we collectively call communication technologies. Warburton examines whether someone who is monogamous but experiences sexual pleasure in virtual reality (and *without* the spouse's participation) commits infidelity. Theano lived long before virtual sex, but her letter to a good friend upset with her husband's affair cautions against letting jealousy and vengeance get the better of her own virtues. Epictetus concisely reviews what most of us have gone through at one time or another, namely, how even the best friendships can be destroyed by one vice or another unleashing its harmful powers. Nyberg, who earlier argued that truth-telling is overrated, here presents the case for deception among good friends as morally permissible under certain conditions.

The last three selections discuss familial love. Plato outlines the case for the state to ensure that parents do rear their biological offspring; whether he is being ironic is something you might discuss with your class. Lin Yutang describes the contrast between the United States and China regarding how they treat and respect the elderly. A recent analysis of the state of the contemporary family in the United States and Western Europe is offered by Midgely and Hughes, who remind us that family life comes in a variety of forms and thrives in a variety of conditions.

40. Case Study: Nancy Mairs, "On Not Liking Sex"

One approach to this essay is reading it as a conversation Mairs conducts with herself. We are the witness. The conversation involves different voices or aspects of Mairs. She switches from the intellectual to the feminist to the victim to the ordinary human being who is confused about him- or herself. The paragraphs inside quotation marks involve the kind of talk one engages in at cocktail parties when trying to impress and shock others. There is some truth to this talk, but Mairs senses that such talk also prevents gaining more substantive insights. Between these paragraphs she reflects on the relation of sex to lust, celibacy, power, politics, and the relation a woman has with her own body. Amid these reflections she talks about her first sexual encounter, a rape by a friend.

The title of the essay bears some attention. You might first ask the students how they understand it. Keep in mind that Mairs is not implying that she dislikes sexual pleasure. Rather, she makes a careful distinction between the desire for sex and the actual experience.

Multiple-Choice Questions

1. Explaining the meaning of her essay's title, Mairs tries to understand the human perversity of
   a. having sex only in secrecy, unlike most animals.
   *b. not wanting what one enjoys.
   c. mixing up pleasure and pain in the heat of passion.
   d. creating codes of sexual conduct that no one obeys.

2. If one looks at human erotic behavior from the angle of war and aggression, then sex is
   *a. tantamount to rape.
   b. a temporary peace treaty.
   c. instinctive, like eating or sleeping.
   d. good only for procreative purposes.

3. When Mairs talks about her tendency toward celibacy, she says the reason is
   a. her love of God.
   b. her fear of getting pregnant again.
   c. the pain of multiple sclerosis that weakens her.
   *d. her fear of love.

Discussion Questions

1. Mairs intersperses her essays with single paragraphs in quotation marks. Select any one of those paragraphs and explain its place in the essay. To what extent do you think the paragraph represents Mairs's genuine thoughts?

2. Why does Mairs say that sex is more than a physical act, that it is a sign with several meanings? What are some of those meanings? Can two persons who have sex with one another have different meanings about what they are doing? According to Mairs or you, do these multiple meanings enhance or diminish human love?

41. St. Augustine, "Lust"

One of the recurring themes in many of our selections is the battle or tension between virtues and vices. Sometimes this battle occurs among various individuals or as part of a larger social controversy. Other times the battle is within oneself. Augustine's reflections on lust is one of the classic statements on the latter. As he puts it, "I came to understand . . . how the *flesh lusts against the spirit and the spirit against the flesh.*"

For those instructors who enjoy presenting selections with some historical background, I have included Augustine's remarks on Antony, the famous early Christian Father who fled to the desert in order to renounce worldly interests. Section VII contains one of Augustine's most celebrated lines when he calls to God, "Grant me chastity and continence, but not yet." It evokes the central tension the self faces in battling lust. Unlike the other vices, lust seems to arise without any cause (e.g., erotic dreams, an attractive person walking by) or recognition by a man's rational faculties. In a word, the power of lust's will eludes the power of the moral will. Hence the "monstrousness" that troubles Augustine in the conclusion, for we see in the self two wills tearing it apart.

In presenting this to students, it is worth noting how God is the anchor of all moral concerns for Augustine. At the same time, for non-religious students Augustine raises some intriguing notions about the self that could be explored in more secular settings. For students interested in questions about date rape, cheating on one's lover, or practicing safe sex, Augustine anticipates answers that involve the idea of self-control and voluntary action. You might ask students whether the current terms such as hormones, genetic tendencies, or aggressive genes are really that much different from Augustine's depiction of the self under siege by contrary forces.

Multiple-Choice Questions

1. For Augustine, the law of sin is
   a. voted upon in democratic societies.
   b. poorly enforced in big cities.
   *c. the fierce force of habit.
   d. a result of hormones out of control.

2. In calling to God, "Grant me chastity and continence, but not yet," Augustine is afraid that
   a. he will never have the chance to have children.
   *b. God will hear his prayer too soon.
   c. he will disappoint his girlfriend.
   d. God does not listen to personal prayers.

3. In talking about his own "monstrousness," Augustine is worried that
   a. his anger at losing self-control is turning him into an animal.
   b. God will turn him into a monster in his next incarnation.
   *c. his mind and body are in conflict.
   d. he is possessed by devil-like monsters.

Discussion Questions

1. What does Augustine mean by the flesh and the spirit against one another? Do you think this conflict is strictly a matter of Augustine's religious or cultural attitude, or do you think his view of the conflict within the self has applications to contemporary life? Give an example to support your answer.

2. How does Augustine understand the power of lust? Describe two or three characteristics of this power. Is Augustine's difficulty in overcoming this power an indicator of a personal weakness or a weakness found in many human beings? Explain your response.

42. Vatsyayana, "Behavior of a Virtuous Woman"

The moral tensions involving lust occur not only within the self. They also appear between persons. The advice for the virtuous woman in the *Kama Sutra* outlines how she should behave toward her husband in various situations. Many students might recoil in disgust or laugh over some of the specific passages. Yet if the examples can be construed not only along the gender lines of an ancient hierarchial attitude but as the contest between contrary interests, choices, or, in the current vernacular, personal lifestyles, students might also see Vatsyayana as offering a solution in which the morality of obedience produces a greater good.

This might be introduced in several ways. Within Vatsyayana's own context, the value of pleasure was one of the central components of the good life; others include duty and enlightenment. The virtuous woman, he concludes, will be both better off and have a husband devoted to her. The contemporary sensibility, of course, assumes that equality and reciprocity should govern human conduct in matters of love. If that is the focus you would like to highlight for your students, then this selection could be a fitting lead-in to the following selections by de Beauvoir and Warburton.

Multiple-Choice Questions

1. When the husband returns from a trip, the virtuous woman should first
   *a. meet him in her ordinary clothes.
   b. embrace him wearing her bedtime outfit.
   c. give him the cold shoulder to show she has not been interested in a man since he left.
   d. order her servants to find out if he had an affair during the journey.

2. If the virtuous woman discovers her husband has misbehaved, she should
   a. use abusive language to him.
   b. blame him excessively.
   c. wait until some friends arrive and then let him have it.
   *d. mildly let him know that she is bothered.

3. Upon hearing women brag about how much their husbands earn, the virtuous wife
   a. inflates her husband's wages so the other wives will be impressed with him.
   b. understates her husband's salary, thus keeping the gossips confused.
   *c. says nothing.
   d. challenges the accuracy of the bragging wives.

Discussion Questions

1. Which do you think anchors the relation between wife and husband in this selection: love, obedience, cultural stereotypes, sexism, or some other idea or belief? Cite passages to support your answer.

2. There is an understandable reaction to dismiss Vatsyayana as an ancient relic. Yet when you hear others jibe one another about a friend being in love and either "hooked," or "being dragged around by a ball and chain," or "under some strange spell," aren't these expressions in part capturing the inequality described by Vatsyayana? Explain why you agree or disagree with this proposal.

43. Simone de Beauvoir, "The Woman in Love"

Another approach to understanding moral struggle in matters of love focuses on the relation between men and women. The passages from de Beauvoir highlight how men and women have a contrary sense of the term "love." Using examples from literature and the social sciences, de Beauvoir depicts love as an existentialist contest in which the lovers are trying to limit or deny the freedom of one another. A key part of this struggle involves how a lover defines not only the other but also oneself. When the man is in love, he still retains a distinct notion of individuality. For him the woman is one of his many values. When the woman is in love, however, a sense of "we" emerges. This "we" includes the woman's idealization of the man, which takes on religious proportions—she sees him as a god. The impossibility of realizing this idealization sets the stage for the recurring conflicts between men and women. If men and women could view genuine love as "founded on the mutual recognition of two liberties," proposes de Beauvoir, then men would not expect to be idealized by women, and women could love out of strength rather than weakness.

It is misleading to say that an existentialist ethic is a variation of virtue ethics. But virtue ethics and existentialism do share an important philosophical concern: what is the scope and dynamic of freedom in human conduct? Whether you wish to emphasize this concern in your class will help you in deciding whether to assign all or part of this selection.

Multiple-Choice Questions

1. Nietzsche is cited early by de Beauvoir because he
   a. is a well-known misogynist.
   b. talks about love while his biographers say he had very little experience in love.
   *c. says that love is not the same thing for a man as it is for a woman.
   d. is rumored to have caught syphilis from a brief fling.

2. Which is NOT an aspect of a woman viewing her man as a god?
   a. she sacrifices her identity
   b. she becomes a devotee seeking salvation
   *c. the man reciprocates by treating her as an angel
   d. the man expects her to recognize his independence

3. For genuine love to be possible, a man and woman should both
   a. be slaves to one another to establish equality.
   *b. be a gift to one another to enrich the world.
   c. declare to one another a manifesto of their individual rights.
   d. contact a lawyer and write up a prenuptial contract.

Discussion Questions

1. What does de Beauvoir mean by freedom? How does she depict the relation between freedom and love? Do you agree or disagree with her views of this analysis?

2. Why does de Beauvoir think that men and women often have a contrary sense of the word "love"? What evidence do you have to support or weaken her case? After considering this evidence, consider whether de Beauvoir offers a realistic ethic about love.

44. Nigel Warburton, "Virtual Fidelity"

The emphasis in this essay is not on the struggle between men and women in love. It is on monogamy, whether homosexual or hetero-sexual. Warburton examines what constitutes infidelity in monogamy in light of a recent phenomenon—virtual reality or cybersex.

His essay first looks at the general risks of nonfidelity (Warburton's term). These include physical, emotional, and relationship risks. He focuses on these risks because he assumes that the morality of an action is assessed by its consequences. Physical risks involve the obvious dangers, such as disease. Emotional risks concern the harms of jealousy and envy. Relationship risks concern the sustained bond of the monogamous couple. Warburton then introduces virtual reality (VR) and the experience of having sexual pleasure while in VR. First he clarifies the extent to which virtual sex is real sex. Then he argues that VR sex does not alone constitute nonfidelity. Indeed, he adds, VR sexual experiences might contribute to rather than detract from a healthy and pleasurable monogamous relationship.

Although some of the points argued by Warburton call for precise distinctions that often are not caught by an introductory student, his attention on VR sex is a topic of interest for many students (not to mention faculty) for whom communications technologies are second nature. The business, cultural, and legal aspects of sexual content in

VR have yet to be settled. Regardless of whether you agree with Warburton, his analysis shows why a philosophical contribution to this controversy is fundamental.

Multiple-Choice Questions

1. Warburton believes people choose monogamy because
    *a. it brings about the best consequences.
    b. they respect traditional religious principles.
    c. the wedding vows are expressions of sacred promises.
    d. they believe monogamy is part of human nature.

2. Another name for virtual reality sex is
    a. "the evil demon," as coined by Descartes.
    b. "fantasy island," according to Roger Scruton.
    c. "hee-haw," as sung by a lead actor on a recent TV show.
    *d. "teledildonics," named by Howard Rheingold.

3. Concluding his essay, Warburton says a VR sex machine is analogous to a
    a. fight simulator, for those who enjoy rough stuff without the bruises.
    *b. flight simulator, for you can operate an airplane without the danger.
    c. bite simulator, for those into nibbles without teeth marks.
    d. lite beer, for it tastes good but is less filling.

Discussion Questions

1. How does Warburton distinguish infidelity from nonfidelity? How does this distinction relate to his discussion about virtual sex? Do you agree with his distinction?

2. Central to his view is the idea that moral issues are determined by their consequences. Insofar as most people fantasize, and virtual sex encourages new avenues for enjoying one's fantasies, virtual sex can nourish rather than threaten a monogamous relationship. Do you believe this is a fair summation of Warburton's argument? If not, what changes would you make? If yes, how do you think you or some of your friends would react if a lover or spouse was discovered having sex via a VR machine?

81

45. Theano, "Letter on Marriage and Fidelity"

This brief letter highlights the love in marriage and the love between friends. Theano cautions her friend Nikostrate from letting her jealousy and vengeance get the better of her virtue. Though understandably upset with her husband's dalliance with a courtesan, Nikostrate's good character must overcome her vicious tendencies. Do not add folly to folly, indecency to indecency, advises Theano. Eventually the husband will return to his senses and appreciate Nikostrate. Furthermore, to act on her jealousy will weaken the marriage and produce benefits for no one.

Despite its brevity and historical distance, the letter contains suggestions and worries that most people go through when seeing friends experience the ups and downs of love or marriage. Asking students about how a moral person helps a friend in this kind of difficulty may be one way of preparing them for this selection.

Multiple-Choice Questions

1. According to Theano, Nikostrate's husband loves the courtesan based on
   a. good judgment.
   b. social status.
   c. bragging rights to his friends.
   *d. passion.

2. The moral faults of her husband will likely cease if Nikostrate
   *a. remains silent.
   b. goes to the courtesan's house and makes a scene.
   c. tells her parents-in-law about the shameful behavior of their son.
   d. nags her husband whenever he comes home.

Discussion Questions

1. If a friend of yours comes to you with a problem similar to Nikostrate's, would your response be similar to or different from Theano's? Briefly explain how you would handle things.

2. Which virtues and vices arise in the circumstances of this letter? To the extent that this involves a moral struggle, which ones do you see as the most important? Specify and elaborate.

46. Epictetus, "Of Friendship"

For many moral thinkers love is the most important of all the virtues. It might also be the most difficult to embrace and practice. Nearly everyone is familiar with the tensions in romantic and erotic love. Friendship seems another matter. For the ancients, friendship rather than erotic love was the exemplary social bond. Yet as Epictetus insightfully observes, even friendships are fragile, vulnerable to the vices that tempt any person.

Epictetus's examples illustrate this fragility. Watch two dogs playing with one another; throw a piece of meat between them and suddenly they start fighting. Note how two siblings enjoy one another throughout their growing up together; show them their possible inheritance and they are ready to kill one another. Epictetus explains the fragility of friendship as due, in part, to ignorance—one gets confused between appearance and substance. Another part of the explanation lies in what the friends value. Is their friendship based on external or tangible things, or is it guided by what the friends value and love in each other's character? As Epictetus puts it, "For where else can friendship be met but with fidelity and modesty, and a communication of virtue; and of no other thing?"

Multiple-Choice Questions

1. In Epictetus's view, a good friendship
   a. lasts forever.
   b. is best secured with a legal agreement.
   *c. can quickly fall apart if the friends are tempted by greed or lust.
   d. is not as good as a solid marriage.

2. Which virtue is best for nourishing a friendship?
   a. pride
   b. hope
   c. faith
   *d. prudence

Discussion Questions

1. What is Epictetus's point in raising the analogy of the dogs playing together? To what extent do you agree or disagree that a true friendship can be assessed according to external and internal goods?

2. As one who has experienced a variety of friendships or read about famous people who suddenly break up with friends or partners, do you believe Epictetus offers an accurate account of the fragility of friendships? Can you think of an alternate explanation? Provide a personal or well-known example to illustrate your answer.

47. David Nyberg, "Friendship and Altruism: Be Untruthful to Others As You Would Have Others Be Untruthful to You"

In Chapter 4 we learned of different disputes on the value of knowledge and whether truthfulness is a virtue. Nyberg's selection criticized those whose moral views on truthfulness tend to overrate it. Does that mean Nyberg also degrades the importance of trust that his opponents believe is essential to truthfulness? Here we see how Nyberg makes an application of his distinction between the value of trust and the value of truthfulness. According to him a good friend can expect—and even prefer—that he or she be deceived by another good friend.

At first glance Nyberg seems to be making an egoistic argument. It puts a lot of weight on an individual's shoulders in terms of deciding when it is right or wrong to lie. There are passages, however, where Nyberg introduces nonegoistic concerns, such as the fundamental interest in maintaining the friendship itself as a distinct or special form of existence. This form does rely on lots of trust, but an act of trust need not always translate into an act of telling the truth. To help see where Nyberg stands, I have included his account of two stories of famous writers who negotiated the truth. They are followed by his main arguments about the relation of truthfulness, trust, and the meaning of friendship. A key part of his argument appears in his claim that we distinguish between trusting a statement and trusting a person.

Multiple-Choice Questions

1. Friends have the right to expect the truth from one another
   *a. except when it takes them to no positive destination.
   b. except when they first agree that they are about to deceive one another.
   c. whenever the issue of love or death arises.
   d. whenever they get too drunk to drive.

2. The point in raising the example of the court jester is made because
   a. Nyberg believes that the court jester always tells the truth to the king.
   b. a critic of Nyberg believes the court jester only amuses the king.
   *c. there is some debate whether the court jester does or should always tell the truth.
   d. Nyberg and his critics agree that the court jester resembles a philosophy professor.

3. For Nyberg, the story on the television program "L.A. Law" shows that Stuart's deception of Abby was NOT an example of
   *a. another sleazy lawyer seducing a troubled woman.
   b. altruistic deception.
   c. an imaginative use of truthfulness.
   d. the gift of friendship.

Discussion Questions

1. Briefly summarize the main points in Nyberg's distinction between trusting the truth and trusting the person. Does he give sufficient reason to his opponents for why they should change their minds? If so, do you now believe that you will accept a friend deceiving you if he or she says your own interests were the primary consideration? Offer an example to explain your position.

2. Nyberg leads off the section with two epigraphs. Choose one and describe its meaning in the context of the selection.

48. Plato, "Communal Families"

The last three selections in this chapter emphasize love and family life. Contrary to those who believe family is strictly a personal or private moral issue, two of the selections also address the social dimensions. In the case of Plato, in fact, the personal ties that characterize the small or biological family can be injurious to social life. His reasoning is that parents tend to take an exaggerated interest in their own children at the expense of concern for the well-being of all children. This fosters an attitude of "my" and "mine" rather than "our." For the good of society's future, a just and responsible state must do all it can to prevent this attitude from prevailing in preparing the young to become virtuous and productive citizens. The festivals with their sacrifices and hymeneal songs are devices of the state to arrange men and women to procreate without learning who their own offspring are. The result will be that parents will treat all children as their own, thus precluding the possibility of possessiveness, jealousy, and vanity that often arise in competitions among families. Discussion of these details is set up by Plato's interest in the training of the state's guardians, who will be both men and women.

Whether to take Plato literally or ironically here is an issue you might raise as students read about the technicalities of the public hymeneals. Certainly some aspects may strike students as hilarious, but understanding the context of the festivals may help them appreciate the philosophical points Plato makes about the morality of love within a family setting. Updating his insights to current discussions about family values and alternative forms of family might be fruitful.

Multiple-Choice Questions

1. When male and female guardians exercise naked, the man who laughs at the woman shows
    a. signs of being a future eunuch.
    b. he's a healthy male.
    c. he's a peasant.
    *d. his own ignorance.

2. A key example to support the state's regulation of procreation is
    a. the caste system in some Hindu countries.
    b. that royalty have never mingled with commoners for marital purposes.
    *c. that animals are bred according to their desired traits.
    d. the downfall of barbarian tribes who neglected the family institution.

3. Which is NOT part of the marriage festivals?
    a. sacrifices
    b. hymeneal songs
    *c. honeymoons
    d. drawing lots for sexual couplings

Discussion Questions

1. To what extent do you think Plato is serious or facetious? Explain your answer in the context of what you think his underlying purpose is in this selection.

2. Do you agree with Plato that the private family threatens the well-being of society because of its narrow and disproportionate focus on its own children? If yes, do you believe his vision of the communal family is the most practical answer? If you think the private family is the best way for rearing children, is this because the private family is simpler, more practical, freer, the locus of genuine love, or some other reason? In your answer specify the points raised by Plato that you find most questionable.

3. Check the weekend newspaper for marriage announcements. How many couples seem to have noticeable points in common, such as education, religion, race, type of job, and so forth? Could one draw the conclusion that people implicitly look at prospective mates in terms of the likely offspring they will produce? If so, then Plato seems to be more candid and rigorous by ensuring that only men and women of similar qualities should mate. Develop your response to this view.

49. Lin Yutang, "Growing Old Gracefully"

A more positive view of love in family life is described by Lin Yutang as the love that includes not only children but aging parents too. Loving one's own children is natural, but loving one's parents as they get old and weak must be taught. For him this is an essential moral lesson. Not to serve one's parents, help them when they are sick, or be with them when they are dying, are sins that can bring shame.

In Lin Yutang's view, this moral regard toward the elderly highlights the most drastic difference between Chinese and Western culture. In the West there is a general fear of the elderly. This can be attributed to the West's traditional emphasis on individualism, neglect of the wisdom that old people can offer, and an odd sort of pride that one's accomplishments are solely of one's own efforts. In a word, what is missing in Western culture is the virtue of gratitude.

This was written in 1931, before Social Security and other government programs were introduced for old people. It might be worth reminding students that as Lin Yutang was writing his reflections on aging, the prototypical image of a destitute and pitiful person in the United States was not the unwed teenage mother or the homeless man begging for quarters at a street corner—it was an old man or woman. That said, Lin Yutang's value of gratitude and being physically near old people still invites important contrasts with how the elderly are viewed today (see Chapter 9 for additional discussions).

Multiple-Choice Questions

1. Which is NOT a moral sin with regard to the elderly in Chinese culture?
   a. neglecting their health
   b. not being present when they are dying
   *c. skimping on financial costs for the funeral
   d. not visiting them or inviting them to your house

2. The moral principle to giving personal service to aging parents rests on
   *a. gratitude.
   b. guilt.
   c. prudence.
   d. pride.

3. People who neglect their aging parents
   a. show foolish individualism.
   b. cheat themselves.
   *c. both of the above.
   d. none of the above.

Discussion Questions

1. Lin Yutang wrote this selection during the time of the great economic depression that struck the United States and much of the world. What do you think he would say about the living conditions of many elderly today? That many receive good health care, travel, and get discounts on a range of services and products could be a sign that Western culture has heeded Lin Yutang's moral advice. Do you agree or disagree with this assessment? Look at his major points to support your answer.

2. Why does Lin Yutang believe people in the West have trouble dealing with old people? Do his reasons capture many of your

experiences and observations about how the elderly are viewed and treated? In his view, do the material comforts old people enjoy translate into a quality of life respected in Chinese culture? Be specific in your answer.

50. Mary Midgely and Judith Hughes, "Trouble with Families?"

The recent controversy over family values or the breakdown in the nuclear family often gets lost amid opposing sides who have an ideological or political ax to grind. Where moral philosophers can help is with a clearer understanding of the problem. Without this effort disputes about the family will continue to waver between nostalgia of a past that never existed and empty rhetoric about opportunities that will soon be missed. Midgely and Hughes conclude this chapter by offering a balanced and thoughtful reflection on the family and its relation to loyalty, love, individualism, and recent trends in modern civilization.

First they remind us of well-known criticisms of the family as the ruin rather than the haven for personal happiness. Plato (see #48), psychiatrists such as R.D. Laing, and sociologists such as Edmund Leach are among many who accuse the family of being "the source of all our discontent." Midgely and Hughes then outline some likely sources for the tensions in modern family life. The emphasis on individualism in liberal democracies and capitalist economies, the increased mobility brought about by machines and job markets, and loose structural supports to ensure that men have continued responsibility for family life all contribute to divorce rates, the increase of single mothers, and geographical separation of the generations.

Finally, Midgely and Hughes admonish all moral thinkers and citizens that if they take family life seriously, then it is both a personal and a social issue.

Multiple-Choice Questions

1. According to psychiatrist R.D. Laing, mental illnesses like neuroses and psychoses are
   a. the result of a dysfunctional family.
   *b. natural responses to typical family life.

c. genetically linked to parents with poorly matched chromosomes.

d. signs that families watch too much violent television.

2. Which have NOT suffered from the rapid increase in modern mobility?
   *a. big businesses
   b. local neighborhoods
   c. church and school organizations
   d. social and political clubs

3. For Midgely and Hughes, the point behind Aristotle's suggestion that men wait until the age of thirty-seven before producing children is that
   a. medical opinion in ancient Greece believed semen to be most potent at that time.
   b. men do not have a stable job before then.
   *c. men need to mature before they take on family responsibilities.
   d. by then they have overcome the Oedipal struggles with their mothers.

Discussion Questions

1. Midgely and Hughes cite a variety of sources condemning the dangers of family life. Select a quote from either Butler, Laing, Larkin, Leach, Godwin, or Epictetus and explain its meaning in the context of the essay and how Midgely and Hughes responded to it. Then consider whether you side with the quote or with the authors.

2. What is Midgely and Hughes's position on the so-called nuclear family (mother and father married to each other, caring for their own offspring)? Do you think their idea of family life would include or exclude such recent suggestions as gay parents, technologically engineered babies, communal families, or no-fault divorces? Explain your answer.

Chapter Review Questions

1. In light of the case study by Mairs, which essays in this chapter do you think offer a similar or contrasting view of the moral importance of love? Select two or three essays and develop a discussion about the struggles involved in living by the principle of love.

2. Do you think all forms of love include some form of possessiveness? Is possessiveness a positive or negative aspect of love? Choose two or three readings to support your position.

3. Although love may not always be a moral beacon for human beings, it seems to be close to a universal experience. Of the readings you have covered in this chapter, which ones: (a) best captured your views on love; (b) most disturbed your views; and (c) gave you new insights. Briefly clarify your reasons.

Chapter 7
Self-Regarding Virtues

A recent news story featured a Nebraska woman who is planning to invite friends and relatives to celebrate her marriage—to herself. She wants to stand in front of a mirror and exchange vows celebrating that she is "happy with herself." Is this a sign that pride is the culmination of the virtuous life? Or is it a symptom of a culture of narcissism in which vanity gets rewarded rather than censured?

The ethical concern persons should have for themselves is a perennial issue. Even though it can be dismissed or trivialized by slogans such as "looking out for Number One," it seems that every moral thinker addresses the importance of self. This was introduced in Chapter 1 with the selections by Browne and Noddings. Here I extend the discussion by including a variety of readings on different aspects of the moral self. Hiriyanna (Chapter 3) reminds us that the moral regard for self and for others should not be viewed as exclusive of one another. Jordan-Smith and Carr characterize this distinction as personal and social virtues. In any event, I take their cue by offering two chapters on the relation between self and other. I hope students do not insist on treating this in dichotomous terms only, but more as a matter of emphasis, for inquiring into these matters involves complex philosophical issues in addition to the more apparent moral ones. As many of the following selections present it, the problem is not just the self but the self's relation to the world. Just as we often disparage or mock the person of hubris, we also pity or commiserate with the person who feels self-contempt. And, as some of the writers remind us, haven't most of us, at one time or another, been the person with hubris or self-contempt?

Kaminer's case study is probably more familiar to students than to teachers. She investigates the talk show circuit, winding up on the Oprah Winfrey program, and recounts with wit and insight the fascination people have in discussing their inner feelings and personal experiences. The selection by Aristotle asserts pride as the crown virtue, for it is the basis for the other virtues to thrive. I have also included how Aristotle distinguishes true pride from excessive and immoral forms of pride. The Dalai Lama views pride as too focused on the individual self and counters Aristotle's position by noting how pride and courage are incompatible.

Sitwell reflects on various notions of pride and humility and draws a compromise. Pride is needed in order to have confidence, she notes, but humility is important to a sense of proportion. The excerpt from Richards's book on humility expounds on the meaning of humility and claims that the humble person is the model for the good life. Humility, says Richards, involves the ability of a moral person to discern how much credit goes to others for one's own accomplishments. Voltaire adds several concise insights about the nature of character and the ordinary or natural value of self-love. Oates richly describes the inner turmoil of those whose relation to the world is so tense and hopeless that despair is the defining experience. To overcome despair and hopelessness, explains Taylor, a healthy sense of self-respect is needed. This self-respect is not an isolated facet but rather an attitude that helps the person overcome the temptations of the vices. Finally, Didion cautions against self-indulgence. But this caution should not go to the opposite extreme—namely, self-alienation.

Presenting the readings in this chapter can probably take several directions. If you or your students believe it to be a central topic, then you might assign all the readings while keeping in mind the nature of the self and the moral importance of self-respect. The discussions on courage and humility could then set up possible counterarguments. If you do not want to be committed to the entire chapter, you might begin with the case study by Kaminer and assign some of the more literary selections by Sitwell, Voltaire, Oates, or Didion. If students are interested, then the more philosophical selections can be assigned. A third approach is to assign a couple of your favorite selections and postpone reading others until you discuss virtues and vices in other chapters. Philosophical discussions on love, caring for others, and burdonsome lives, for example, invariably bring attention back to the understanding of self.

51. Case Study: Wendy Kaminer, "Testifying: Television"

This selection is from Kaminer's book on the popularity of self-analysis, particularly with the apparent delight Americans have in talking about being victims and living in dysfunctional settings. Although a number of her astute observations could have been used for a case study, this one includes several features worth raising in an ethics course. Celebrities as well as ordinary people are brought together. Confession and testimony are introduced as part of a cultural tradition, even though the religious and psychiatric contexts are given a new twist by talk shows. The concern with self-knowledge, self-help, and self-esteem are rendered as public services or altruistic deeds since some viewer may be helped by watching someone on TV talking about his suffering from Peter Pan syndrome or lamenting her codependency. Finally, although most of us snicker at talk shows from a comfortable distance, Kaminer actually appears on one. And she confesses that staying in a first-class hotel and being chauffeured in a limo to the Oprah show made her feel like Cinderella. The selection is easily accessible except for her use of the term "postmodern." Although "postmodern" has become an umbrella term covering all sorts of eclectic meanings, you might briefly sketch for students your sense of the term.

Multiple-Choice Questions

1. The spectacle of watching strangers tell their sordid tales is NOT a sign of
   a. voyeurism.
   *b. the decline of commercial television.
   c. sham communities.
   d. exhibitionism.

2. In talk show language, "victims of a disease process" are
   *a. gluttons.
   b. suffering from a sexual disease because they cannot control their lust.
   c. being treated for nervous disorders caused by excessive stress and anger.
   d. slothful.

3. Appearing on Oprah, Kaminer and fellow guests are encouraged by an assistant to behave
   a. as if they are in a college seminar.
   b. like guests do on Jerry Springer, and come out swinging.
   c. like guests do on a Public Broadcasting program.
   *d. as if they are at a large, unruly family dinner on Thanksgiving.

Discussion Questions

1. Do you believe talk shows can offer some lessons about moral values and conduct? Using Kaminer's observations as a guide, select two or three samples from different current programs and examine to what extent they merely pretend to address serious issues or actually make some genuine contributions to moral concerns. Be specific in describing the material presented by the hosts, guests, and even the audience.

2. Can television as a medium contribute to moral improvement? Although Kaminer notes an occasional exception, for the most part she portrays talk shows as spectacles in which viewers want to be amused and stimulated and concludes that these viewers are afraid of boredom and are unwilling to reflect on values and thoughts. In light of the tone of her observations, to what extent do you think television improves, corrupts, or is neutral to moral development?

52. Aristotle, "Pride As the Crown Virtue"

One problem raised by Kaminer is that notions of self-esteem and self-respect are used so often that people lose sight of their value or meaning. The selection by Aristotle attempts some clarification by emphasizing the importance of pride and its relation to the good life. He outlines how the proud person is careful to avoid excesses that appear as pride but are not. Bragging, vanity, and false humility give genuine pride a bad name. Moreover, a proud person enjoys accomplishments and honors but does not use them to belittle others or to seek the flattery of others. Except for friendship, the proud person seeks independence.

In gaining a sense of Aristotle's view of pride, one can understand his disparaging remarks on its excesses. Vain people are fools, unduly humble people are ignorant, and the braggart is contemptible. Aristotle's reasons generally have to do with how those suffering from excessive pride have a distorted view of themselves, hence they are unreliable or untrustworthy in matters of truthfulness and social interaction.

How thoroughly you cover this selection will likely depend on whether you emphasize the historical or philosophical approaches to virtues and vices. For Aristotle the virtues that he recommended were not always universal in scope. The man of honor had certain distinctions in terms of class and education that reflect a hierarchal society. (Indeed, in Aristotle's time slavery was common and women had second-class status.) These points need not dictate your presentation of Aristotle. Keep in mind that Alisdair MacIntyre, among others, believes the moral principles of Aristotle can be extracted from historical circumstances to form the basis for virtue ethics in contemporary life.

Multiple-Choice Questions

1. According to Aristotle, the proud man is most concerned with
   a. honor, because it brings the greater goods of power and wealth.
   b. power, since it brings respect from others that gives pride practical value.
   c. honor, but only if it is free of power and wealth.
   *d. honor, even if it does bring power and wealth.

2. The unduly humble man
   *a. does not know himself.
   b. is the best antidote to vanity.
   c. knows himself better than the proud man knows himself.
   d. is a moral exemplar.

3. The buffoon is NOT
   a. a slave to his sense of humor.
   *b. tactful.
   c. well-bred.
   d. respectful of anything that might be occasion for a joke.

Discussion Questions

1. From your reading of Aristotle, can everyone be proud in his sense of the term? Why, or why not?

2. Using Aristotle's own names and classifications, how would you describe some of the guests on talk shows? Can you apply his classifications to those you encounter in your own life? You might consider different settings, such as school, work, parties, home or dormitory, sports teams, or social organizations.

53. Dalai Lama, "On Pride, Courage, and Self"

This selection comprises lectures the Dalai Lama presented at Harvard. It is somewhat lengthier than the average selection. In light of the original format you can easily assign individual lectures, depending on how thoroughly you want to contrast Aristotle with the Dalai Lama—two famous names representing enduring systems of thought—give some philosophical or religious background to the Tibetan Buddhist view of the virtuous self, or add some meaningful thoughts by the Dalai Lama whose familiarity to students might be based solely on a recent Hollywood movie or rock concerts devoted to the freedom of his native land.

The excerpt on the source of suffering gives a concise account of karma and introduces the "ultimate virtue"—the "true cessation of a level of suffering." Here he also distinguishes deliberate and non-deliberate actions and correlates them with different levels of virtue. In the "Question and Answer" passage the Dalai Lama contrasts pride and courage. Pride gives the self the feeling of importance, independence, and substance. But this mode of thought differs from that mode that belongs to courage, the virtue that encourages people to "respectfully hold others to be supreme." The theme of the self and non-self is continued in "True Paths." In this excerpt he talks about the "ethics of the abandonment of the non-virtues." These nonvirtues take three forms: physical (e.g., stealing), verbal (e.g., senseless chatter), and mental (e.g., covetousness). This abandonment involves a kind of liberation, but this too can be prevented by such vices as anger, according to the Dalai Lama. This is followed by the lecture on altruism where he elaborates on the struggle between anger or hatred and love or compassion. At stake in this struggle are happiness and wisdom, particularly the wisdom that the human individual self is no more nor less important than another human or living creature. This point is concisely put in the last excerpt, "Bodhisattva Deeds," whose root of ethics is "the restraining of self-centeredness."

I have arranged these presentations in a tentative sequence. Summarizing some of the selections could allow you to assign other selections you think are most important. Or you might wait to see how much students are interested in reading the thoughts of someone who has become something of a surprise celebrity.

Multiple-Choice Questions

1. The ultimate virtue is
   a. faith.
   b. introspection.
   *c. cessation of suffering.
   d. pride.

2. Courage is entirely different from
   a. cowardice.
   b. sloth.
   c. envy.
   *d. pride.

3. After a trial of celibacy, according to the Highest Yoga Tantra, a wise person engages in sexual union because
   a. of suppressed lust.
   b. ritualistic orgies followed the trials.
   *c. a higher path to truth may be gained.
   d. of pride.

4. Tolerance or patience can best be learned from
   *a. an enemy.
   b. your guru.
   c. sloth.
   d. pride.

Discussion Questions

1. How is the Dalai Lama's view of self different from more familiar views? Outline three or four basic features of the Tibetan Buddhist view and a more familiar view? What do you see as notable differences? How are they morally relevant?

2. Many selections have illustrated the relation of virtues with other virtues and vices. How would you explain to someone not taking this course the key structure of this relation in the perspective of the Dalai Lama? If you were to use a metaphor, would the "ladder" described by Jordan-Smith (Chapter 3) be helpful, or can you imagine a more informative metaphor or image? Be specific in your answer.

54. Edith Sitwell, "Pride"

Sitwell presents an ambivalent portrayal of pride. There are times when it certainly gets the better of us; and, as many classic literary pieces show, a perennial tragic-comedy is the experience of fallen pride. But more often, Sitwell observes, pride is a valuable component of the good life. As epitomized in the 1959 story about a town's plan to lock a man in a cage for eight days as part of a public carnival, with feeding times posted by his cage, the debasement of a human being's pride is hideous, writes Sitwell. As with Aristotle and the Dalai Lama, Sitwell's discussion includes trying to understand the relation between pride and humility. She adroitly notes how some of the greatest writers and thinkers have wrestled with this relation.

This is one of several contributions in this chapter from nonphilosophers; how to present this to students partly depends on their ability to catch some of the literary anecdotes spicing up Sitwell's reflections. Don't forget that she does conclude with an argument from Epiharnus that begins with "I am a corpse" and concludes with "(I am) a God."

Multiple-Choice Questions

1. When she was twenty-two years old, Sitwell learned a lesson about pride from
   a. her boyfriend.
   *b. a peacock.
   c. a lion.
   d. Aristotle.

2. For Sitwell one should take pride not only as an individual but for
   *a. humanity.
   b. all sentient creatures.
   c. struggling artists.
   d. poor people.

Discussion Questions

1. How does Sitwell understand the relation between pride and humility? Which examples best illustrate her understanding?

2. Why do you think Sitwell emphasizes the importance of pride for the artist? Do you think she has a special affinity for artists

that devalues the importance of pride for nonartists? Or do you feel her notion of artist can be extended to most people? Clarify your response.

55. Norvin Richards, "The Virtue of Humility"

Richards gives a philosophical elaboration of Sitwell's points by clarifying how humility offers the antidote not so much to pride but to the vices that come from pride, such as jealousy and anger. His observations on keeping a sense of proportion about the importance of self also deserve comparison with the Dalai Lama.

Much of his emphasis is on understanding oneself in relation to others and the world. There is an almost natural tendency, notes Richards, to overstate the harms that happen to me while understating the suffering of others. In addition, there is a desire to receive attention or benefits for myself that either are not fully deserved or are more justly offered to others. Letting these dispositions shape one's moral attitudes and conduct can threaten pursuit of the good life. To prevent these dangers, a restored sense of humility is fundamental. Unfortunately, writes Richards, humility has suffered a worse reputation than pride. People tend to associate humility with passivity, meekness, or a false sense of modesty. Genuine humility is more positive. It can be a guide toward justice, confidence, and self-understanding. If one interprets the Delphic Oracle's maxim, "Know Thyself," as a call to understand one's own limits, then we might say Richards presents an updated version by calling attention to the dangers of self-absorption.

He closes the selection with some practical observations: how a humble person decides how much credit is deserved for one's own accomplishments; when humility frees us from elitism and enables us to appreciate others; that humility diminishes paternalism and enhances tolerance. In my view, if you are planning on devoting considerable attention to the ideas in this chapter, then the Richards selection could easily be the centerpiece around which the other readings are discussed.

Multiple-Choice Questions

1. Two vices that humility helps us overcome are
   *a. anger and envy.
   b. lust and sloth.

     c.   gluttony and greed.

     d.   sloth and gluttony.

2.   To walk up a secluded hillside and take pride in the lovely view is

     a.   sensible, since you used your physical powers to reach the top of the hill.

     b.   properly humble, because it reflects your ability to judge beautiful things.

   *c.   strange, for you can't take credit for the hillside being there.

     d.   false modesty if you are really thinking that you are the king of the hill.

Discussion Questions

1.   How does Richards distinguish the virtues of humility from the vices of pride? List the features of each, offering an example to highlight your understanding. Do you agree that humility's virtues contribute to the good life?

2.   A humble person knows how much credit is deserved for one's accomplishments, says Richards. Is this possible? Consider one of your accomplishments (or failures): to what extent can you accurately discern who gets the credit (or blame)? If this cannot be discerned, is Richards offering an impractical ethic?

56. Voltaire, "Character" and "Self-Love"

Virtue ethics emphasizes the importance of moral character. But what exactly is character? Although a number of thinkers focus on the development of good habits, the rational control over dangerous tendencies, or the discipline to withstand temptations as central aspects of moral character, Voltaire presents a more skeptical view of character. Briefly, he doubts that we have much say over the kind of person nature has made us. Just as nature gives us certain physical features and specific talents over which we have no control, so too it gives us qualities that we can do little to change. Contrary to most moralists, Voltaire does not expect rational inquiry to help matters. "If one does not reflect, one thinks oneself master of everything; but when one does reflect, one realizes that one is master of nothing," he notes. His examples support this position. When one's character does change, he adds, this has less to do with personal morality and is more the result of aging or external contingencies.

The selection on self-love concisely explains that pride is a natural attribute. With his usual wit, Voltaire notes how self-love is essential to the species and gives us pleasure, but "it has to be hidden." This last point provides a possible challenge to the treatises on humility insofar as we may never be sure when this virtue is self-love in the best disguise.

Multiple-Choice Questions

1. When the ninety-year-old man chastises the young men's behavior with some girls, Voltaire's point is that the old man
   a. offers himself as a moral example.
   *b. deceives himself.
   c. helps the young men to practice safe sex.
   d. is envious that he is no longer a virile man.

2. The Indian fakir having himself whipped was
   a. engaging in kinky sex.
   b. practicing self-denial.
   *c. preparing himself for life in the next world.
   d. punishing himself for his own sins.

Discussion Questions

1. How does Voltaire's etymology of "character" reflect his belief that there is little we can do to change our character? Explain your views on his position.

2. What is his view on self-love? How does it compare with other views, such as those offered by the Dalai Lama, Richards, Sitwell, or others you have covered in this chapter? Do you think some of the people on talk shows reflect Voltaire's sense of self-love? Develop your own views of the meaning and value of self-love in light of Voltaire's observations.

57. Joyce Carol Oates, "Despair"

Another candidate for the list of sins is despair. Its dangerous powers can threaten anyone. Most of us experience some despair at one time or another. But despair at its most dangerous is hard to confront because it involves the moral person's own disregard for self. Is this disregard due to the blissful realization of the no-self? Or is this disregard attributable to painful hatred of oneself?

Oates richly describes how someone could explain the right answer to the second question. Yet she also realizes that to fully explain or understand despair is problematic. Despair represents such an independent and deep turn to an inward self that its core experience might be impossible to articulate. Given how Voltaire sees self-love as natural and pleasant, Oates raises evidence showing how frequent the opposite appears. Some of those who best expressed a real sense of despair capture a rich variety of human experiences where self-loathing is almost celebrated, at least in some of our greatest writers. Oates cites them as best able to portray the meaning of despair. Kafka, Nietzsche, and Dickinson are some of the writers discussed by Oates. Yet, she adds, the beauty of their writing in some ways helps us transcend or resist despair. In that sense the confrontation with despair can sink us, she acknowledges. But she reminds us that in this confrontation one also finds, as she does in Dickinson's "Carrion Comfort," a "statement of humankind's strength, and not weakness."

This essay could be handled in several ways: as part of general discussions of material in this chapter, as a distinct contrast with the Dalai Lama on the value of experiencing the no-self, or as a plausible candidate for one of the principal vices (or deadly sins). In any event, as this anthology was emerging, this selection by Oates was considered "necessary." At the time I did not know of Oates's stature in literary circles and popular forums. It was just serendipity to find this when I was looking for material on the seven deadly sins. Read her essay from a student's point of view and you should see why I still consider this to be one of the essential readings in the text.

Multiple-Choice Questions

1. According to Oates, the antipode or exact opposite of American enthusiasm is
    a. William James.
    b. Herman Melville.
   *c. Emily Dickenson.
    d. the cynical college professor.

2. The most sinful deed attached to despair is
    a. murder.
   *b. suicide.

c.   torture.

d.   taking a course from a cynical college professor.

3.   Part of Oates's appreciation of Kafka's portrayal of despair lies in

*a.   its humor.

b.   his religious sincerity.

c.   her own experience of changing into a giant cockroach.

d.   its verifiability.

Discussion Questions

1.   How does Oates explain the relation of poetry to despair? Do you think other artists or voices can provide an insight into the dangers of despair? Cite some examples in order to clarify your understanding of the degrees of despair.

2.   Oates suggests that the best teachers of despair are the poets and literary writers. Select one of these writers' quoted passages that interests you and discuss how it belongs in the essay. What is your understanding of the passage?

58. Gabriele Taylor, "Deadly Vices?"

If Oates rather than, say, Richards or the Dalai Lama is your focal point in this chapter, then Taylor gives a valuable philosophical elaboration of the points raised by Oates. Taylor's point of departure for understanding the despairing self does not dwell on suicide, however, but on the dangers of sloth or acedia (see Jordan-Smith, Chapter 3, and Pynchon, Chapter 10). As with many of the selections, she presents this problem as a struggle between virtues and vices. In this case, the best counter to sloth or acedia is self-love. As a virtue, self-love best opposes sloth because it embraces a feeling of engagement with the world and a sense of confidence and enjoyment with oneself.

Taylor begins by outlining three familiar dimensions of virtues. There is the class of social virtues, a class of other-regarding virtues, and finally there are self-regarding virtues. Again, as with earlier thinkers on this classification scheme, the distinctions are more a matter of emphasis than of exclusivity. Taylor's emphasis is on sloth as a self-regarding problem. Mindful of the history of sloth (or acedia) as a key religious vice, Taylor nevertheless elucidates its current threats to the self in mostly secular terms. These threats can be generally grouped under the idea of indolence or boredom. Boredom has many manifestations. Some are quite harmless, such as being bored with a task at work, a school assignment, or a faculty meeting. But when boredom is "objectless," it signals a "mood-state" that demands our moral consideration.

Taylor's distinctions between mood and emotion, despair and hopelessness as daughters of acedia, and occurrent and standing moods are finely drawn and may elude introductory students. I have included her entire essay to give students and instructors the opportunity to see how her descriptions of boredom and acedia fit her larger view. If you want to focus on self-love as a virtue that struggles against the deadly vices, you might assign or summarize passages from the first part of the essay and from section IV.

Multiple-Choice Questions

1. You can tell a slothful person by
   a. observing his behavior.
   *b. understanding her state of mind.
   c. measuring the percentage of idle hours to working hours.
   d. inquiring if he or she is spiritually dead.

2. According to Taylor, self-deception
   a. is a moral way of overcoming suffering.
   *b. prevents a person from becoming complete.
   c. is natural, so let it flourish as long it does not bother anyone.
   d. happens only to those suffering from vanity.

3. The virtue best able to oppose sloth is
   a. industriousness, as introduced by Benjamin Franklin.
   b. self-love, as expressed in self-indulgence.
   c. love of a divine being, as the medieval philosophers believed.
   *d. self-love, as expressed in self-concern.

Discussion Questions

1. What does Taylor mean by sloth? What makes it a dangerous vice? Do you observe slothful persons in the movies, magazines, or your own experiences? Do they fit Taylor's moral assessment?

2. How does Taylor's view of self-love compare and contrast to more ordinary notions of self-love? Does her clarification of self-love offer the best opposition to sloth? Explain your answer.

59. Joan Didion, "On Self-Respect"

Concluding this chapter is a concise and thoughtful reflection on moral character that is the source for self-respect. Didion does not claim to be breaking new ground. Self-respect is a venerable value taught to us by well-known writers, famous thinkers, and even our grandparents. It has to do with taking responsibility for one's own actions rather than seeking scapegoats. Avoiding this kind of responsibility is easy, hence Didion's point that self-respect develops a certain toughness in a person. The appeal of her essay is in how she argues that self-respect is the key to living by other virtues. The person without self-respect might be harmless enough, but he or she suffers something profound—self-alienation.

Multiple-Choice Questions

1. People with self-respect have the courage
    a. to give up their lives for others.
    b. to commit sins without guilt.
    *c. of their mistakes.
    d. to admit that in the larger scheme of things individual lives don't matter.

2. An important lesson for Didion in learning about self-respect was
    a. receiving a prestigious literary award.
    *b. not getting into Phi Beta Kappa.
    c. finally getting the approval of her colleagues.
    d. recovering from a codependency therapy session.

Discussion Questions

1. Didion's emphasis on self-respect is part of a traditional moral lesson of responsibility. Why do you think Didion thinks it is important to raise this as a virtue in the last part of the twentieth century? Note that she wrote this in the 1960s; to what extent do her words still apply?

2. Why does Didion address self-deception? Can you have self-deception and self-respect at the same time? Why, or why not?

3. Didion does not say much about other-regarding or social virtues. Do you believe this could simply be a matter of space and emphasis, or do you think her understanding of self-respect treats it as more important than other-regarding or social virtues? Explain your response.

Chapter Review Questions

1. Voltaire says self-love is natural. If so, then why is there so much discussion about the morality of self-love? Select two or three of the readings to develop your understanding about the relative importance of self-love in terms of pride, humility, self-respect, despair, or another value raised in the reading.

2. How do the epigraphs by the Delphic Oracle and Wendy Kaminer introduce discussion of self-regarding virtues? Specifically, what is the relation between knowing oneself, talking about oneself, and loving or respecting oneself? Consider four possibilities: (a) if you love yourself, then you know yourself; (b) if you do not talk about yourself, then you do not love yourself; (c) if you know yourself, then you should love yourself; and (d) loving or respecting yourself and knowing yourself are not directly related. Which of the four (or can you propose a fifth?) do you support or reject? Explain, using relevant passages from any of this chapter's readings to clarify your answer.

Chapter 8
Morality and the Other

We have already seen a number of references to other-regarding virtues. There's the risk of treating these references as involving a vague notion of altruism. The ordinary or popular media view of altruism usually involves dramatic heroism or saintly self-denial. Important as these connotations might be, they tend to be exceptionable in terms of everyday moral experiences or habits. Can there be a moral regard for the other that offers more substantive components while avoiding the trap of appealing only to the episodic illustrations of altruism?

The selections chosen here address this question in concrete discussions. Rather than emphasize the theoretical debates about the relation between self and other, the essays in this chapter orient their moral interest in the other by talking first about moral concerns for specific others. By organizing the selections in clusters of three, however, I hope to show that the initial concern for a specific other can foster important philosophical inquiries.

The case study by Berrigan meditates about helping those who are dying of AIDS and other causes. This is followed by three selections on the care ethic. Noddings argues for the historical and philosophical support of the virtue of caring for those who are suffering or in need. It has been embodied by women in all cultures for a morally good reason—it enables society to flourish. Hoagland's rejoinder focuses on Noddings's misleading portrayal of the woman as happily developing her moral talents to help others. Rather, the care ethic takes advantage of women while they and everyone else neglect the well-being of women. Carse and Nelson believe the basic points made by Noddings are valid, and their response to her critics is that the care ethic is both positive and universal—that is, applicable to women as well as men.

The next cluster of selections addresses the environmental ethic, which is concerned with the other as characterized by a range of terms, such as nature, biosphere, Gaia, or ecosystem. In terms of our treatment of animals, says Racy, it is a matter of justice that humans should treat animals as near moral equivalents. Shaw expands this view to include a respect for all the land. This respect can be attained by embracing three virtues—prudence, honesty, and thoughtfulness. The rejoinder by Cronon reviews the recent history of American thought about wilderness and nature. What we learn from this history is that many environmentalists, regardless of their intentions, forget that the concern for nature does not respect it as truly other; rather, they like nature insofar as it is tamed and no longer strange, scary, or wild.

The final cluster of selections evoke a devotion to the other that is intangible yet greater than oneself. For Royce this is rooted in the virtue of loyalty to a cause, movement, or belief. Loyalty rather than self-regard is the anchor to the moral life. Hildegard von Bingen recounts her vision on how the effect of divine love generates a creative experience. From visioning and hearing the signs of spiritual others such as angels and devils, Hildegard articulates the virtues of love, humility, and peace. The selection from Plato (and others in this chapter too) could have been placed in Chapter 6, but I included it here to draw attention to the moral regard for that which is not easily recognizable, namely, the regard for the love, truth, or beauty discovered in the other. In this discovery the self is brought to other-worldly concerns.

How to present this chapter is largely a matter of either familiarity with the issues, sense of student interest, or your own interest in the growing humanities discussion on the meaning of the other (or alterity). If you want to focus on arguments and counterarguments, the selections on the care ethic or environmental ethic can be assigned. They are also topical. If you want to introduce students to these topics, following the Berrigan case study with Carse and Nelson and Racy should be adequate. The cluster of Hildegard, Royce, and Plato is largely a judgment call. I have included them in part due to their beautiful pronouncements on their respective values. They are also included because the love of a deity, a cause, or a truth has probably produced as much good—and harm—as anything loved by humans that is not like themselves.

60. Case Study: Daniel Berrigan, "In the Evening We Will Be Judged by Love"

The regard for others who are not like ourselves involves some philosophical disputes about the nature of the other. Here we are considering the moral attitude toward others as recognizing: first, that they may not resemble us in terms of a common language, nationality, economic or cultural background, shared interests, or life's goals; second, that the anticipation of reciprocity or equivalent exchange is void; and third, that the other is one who makes an appeal to us in his or her suffering or need. Obviously, each of us can be an other to someone else.

The case study by Berrigan illustrates these points in his help with those who are dying. He is often called by parishioners, acquaintances, or friends to attend to someone who they know is dying. Berrigan is sometimes called as a last resort, for no one else seems to have the strength or willingness to visit and really talk with the dying person. It is not an easy task, Berrigan acknowledges, but the courage—not to mention humor—shown by the dying often help him.

Multiple-Choice Questions

1. Berrigan learns from the dying Luke that he was NOT
   a. a master chef.
   b. dying from AIDS.
   c. the peacemaker in his family.
   *d. an Irish freedom fighter.

2. The virtue Berrigan learns from Luke and others who are dying is
   *a. courage.
   b. prudence.
   c. pride.
   d. justice.

Discussion Questions

1. Why is attending the dying so difficult? Is the reluctance to be with the dying a sign of weakness, fear, practicality, or moral ineptitude? Or do you think there should be no moral significance attached to attending the dying? Explain your answer.

2. What does Berrigan learn from those who know death awaits them? Does Berrigan suggest that everyone learn how to help the dying? Why, or why not?

61. Nel Noddings, "Caring"

In Chapter 1 Noddings outlined her view of relational ethics. Here she develops her more widely known view of the care ethic. Although some commentators believe the care ethic is a modern-day notion of religious charity without religion, Noddings argues that the virtue of care has a distinct place in moral thought. Its significance includes its being both a personal and a social virtue. Although caring has long been associated with women and hence devalued in comparison with more assertive virtues, according to Noddings, caring, when properly understood, actually embraces courage. Caring also better counters the dangerous tendencies of the self-regarding moral attitudes by reminding us that all of us at one time or another seek or need to be cared for by someone else. The problem with recognizing the legitimacy of the care ethic lies in the self-deception and short-sighted pride that allow individualistic ethics to focus on rights and laws as the anchor to the moral life.

I have included a fairly long selection from Noddings's book. Many students are majoring in or already work in a helping profession. Many of them may have a sick relative who needs their attention. The philosophical lessons from these experiences are addressed by Noddings in a thorough review of central moral issues, such as the nature of right and wrong, the traditional emphasis on judging actions rather than persons, and the search for absolutes in complicated dilemmas. If you want to highlight her key points, you might assign the introductory section and the "Women and Morality: Virtue" and "Toughness of Caring" sections.

Multiple-Choice Questions

1. The difference between natural caring and ethical caring is that
   a. natural caring is for those you like, ethical caring is for those you do not like.
   b. the former is found in animals only, and the latter in humans.
   c. women illustrate natural caring but only mothers show ethical caring.
   *d. natural caring is based on sentiment, whereas ethical caring has memory and effort.

2. The biblical story about the rich man who ignored the beggar Lazarus represents
   a. justice in the care ethic, since the rich man eventually suffered eternal torment.
   *b. the harsh judgment of masculine ethics.
   c. an early form of socialism.
   d. the uselessness of pity.

3. Morality that is based on laws is, according to Noddings,
   a. useless.
   *b. of limited use.
   c. of the greatest use if the laws are written by women.
   d. of the greatest use if they include penal codes for those who do not care.

Discussion Questions

1. How does Noddings understand the relation between love and the care ethic? Do you think she is offering a variation of the golden rule or a distinct moral outlook?

2. What is meant by masculine approaches to ethics? Why does Noddings criticize them? Select one example of a masculine ethic and show how its approach to a moral dilemma differs from the approach used by one embracing the virtue of care. Be specific.

62. Sarah Lucia Hoagland, "Some Thoughts about Caring"

Although Hoagland appreciates Noddings's efforts in proposing a distinct feminist ethic, as a feminist she finds several noticeable shortcomings with the care virtue. Unwittingly, perhaps, Noddings portrays the moral contributions of women from a man's rather than a woman's point of view. Of course men will celebrate the care ethic—it is to their benefit. If men were doing the caring, it likely would not be recognized as a positive moral trait. Related to this fallacy is Noddings's inadequate portrayal of the one who does the caring. According to Hoagland, the one who cares generally is inferior to the one cared for (such as the slave caring for the master), and this status is reinforced due to the one-directional nature of the care ethic. From these two flaws it follows that the care ethic as formulated by Noddings is inadequate for dealing with social and political injustice because it is too oriented to caring for a familiar person. Hence, the conditions are set up so that strangers are excluded from care, contends Hoagland. She proposes a more radical view than Noddings, one based not on the mother but on the amazon as the model of a moral life.

Grasping much of this essay depends on being familiar with the features of the care virtue. Assigning sections of Noddings or giving a summary of her views should help students understand Hoagland's critique. If you are mostly interested in Hoagland's main points, the introduction and the section on "Insularism" might suffice if you fill in the gaps.

Multiple-Choice Questions

1. Hoagland believes the care virtue
    *a.   reestablishes women's dependence on men.
    b.   liberates women from men.
    c.   makes all humans equal.
    d.   should rank lower than laws as the basis for moral life.

2. A preferable model for the moral life, according to Hoagland, is
    a.   the single mother.
    *b.   an amazon.
    c.   a celibate woman.
    d.   any woman from a non-Western culture.

3. Heterosexualism is NOT about
    a.   men disliking women.
    *b.   men and women liking each other.
    c.   normalizing the dominance of one person over another.
    d.   undermining female agency.

Discussion Questions

1. Hoagland says Noddings's moral exemplar of one who cares reflects "a lack of experience with the world" and a "withdrawal from the public domain." What do these points mean? How might Noddings respond? Do you agree or disagree with Noddings or Hoagland?

2. What are the main features to Hoagland's moral alternative? Do you think it is preferable to either Noddings's or other moral examples? Explain your answer.

63. Alisa L. Carse and Hilde Lindemann Nelson, "Rehabilitating Care"

This defense of the basic points made by Noddings acknowledges that the care ethic could pose the risk of exploitation of the care giver. Carse and Nelson also grant the historical evidence that women have been taken advantage of when caring is always one-directional. But these dangers are not inevitable. Contrary to feminist and legal critics of the care virtue, there is good reason to believe that Noddings has provided the ethical framework from which personal morality and social justice can be understood and pursued.

Part of Carse and Nelson's defense of Noddings focuses on the meaning of the care giver–recipient dyad. Critics contend that the inequality of this dyad is ripe for exploitation of the giver. Carse and Nelson point out, however, that the dyad does not occur in isolation; it is part of a cluster of social relations. If an adult woman is taking care of her sister suffering from Alzheimer's and seems exploited, it is likely that the sister is *not* the culprit. Rather, the care giver's burdens are likely neglected by other siblings, her husband and children, and even friends. If the care giver's other relations recognized her distinct needs while she tries to provide for the ailing sister, then Carse and Nelson believe the care ethic would be practiced in varying degrees by everyone in the community. This could be a microcosm of the care ethic in a larger community, hence the emergence of a sense of social justice.

In their view, other theories do not fully appreciate the singular characteristics of each care situation. Feminists critical of the care virtue simplify the care ethic by extracting the dyad from the web of social relations that comprise our everyday experiences. Additional observations by Carse and Nelson include that the mother-child model is not the only moral paradigm for the care ethic and that, properly understood, Noddings's view of caring can be extended to the stranger. The result, they conclude, is that instead of proposing a more radical version of a feminist ethic we should be constructing a "degendering of the care ethic." In this sense it becomes the basis for a universal morality. As with the Noddings and Hoagland selections, parts of this essay can be technical. If your main purpose is to introduce students to some disputes in feminist ethics, you might cover the entire essay. If you hope that students appreciate the intellectual tensions over a new candidate for a fundamental virtue, you could assign the beginning and closing sections of this essay.

Multiple-Choice Questions

1. Which criticism of the care ethic is NOT addressed by Carse and Nelson?
   a. It unfairly favors the mother-child dyad.
   b. It lacks an adequate social justice.
   *c. The model of the amazon is a better alternative.
   d. Care givers are exploited.

2. Relationships among people who care for one another are bound together by
   *a. trust.
   b. law.
   c. custom.
   d. mutual enslavement.

3. Rehabilitating the care ethic means it should be extended to include
   a. people who do not hold an academic degree.
   b. fathers.
   c. women of all economic and social classes.
   *d. men.

Discussion Questions

1. Hoagland charges Noddings with using a model of care that lacks everyday experience in the world. Carse and Nelson counter with the point that the care ethic is rooted in a web of ordinary but complex social relations. What does each side mean? Who do you think is correct, and why?

2. What is meant by caring for strangers? Is it practical to expect the caring virtue to better help others than, say, laws of justice or economic policies? Elaborate your views by citing relevant passages from Noddings, Hoagland, or Carse and Nelson.

64. Ray Racy, "In Justice to Animals"

The next three selections address an issue that has become fairly popular with students as well. However, the popularity of various environmental causes is often based on erratic or sentimental concerns. Some are against animal experimentation but are not vegetarians; some hate zoos but keep their own pets confined indoors; many are upset with pollution but buy cars that average less than fifteen miles a gallon. The following selections raise the stakes somewhat by addressing some philosophical and historical aspects of environmental ethics.

Racy reviews the case for treating animals and other natural entities as morally equivalent to humans. Applying general principles such as utilitarian regard for suffering and the golden rule, Racy concludes that animals have as much right to have their interests respected as humans. For him it is more than a matter of sentimentality or compassion—it is a matter of justice. Once this has been established, then the subsequent task for moral people is to find ways of carrying out this principle of justice.

Multiple-Choice Questions

1. Animals should have their moral rights respected because
   a. humans ought to show care for sentient creatures completely different from themselves.
   *b. they are more similar to humans than we realize.
   c. the Bible was wrong in proclaiming that humans have dominion over nature.
   d. they are cuter and more cuddly than most humans.

2. Racy quotes Bentham in order to emphasize that animals
   a. have rational capacities.
   b. use language.
   c. are capable of self-reflection.
   *d. can suffer.

3. That animals cannot speak on their own behalf is irrelevant, says Racy. Which humans are NOT included for their inability to speak on their own behalf?
   a. mental defectives
   b. children
   *c. guests on the Jerry Springer show
   d. primitive tribes

Discussion Questions

1. After reading Racy's essay, list two or three features that make animals and humans different; then list two or three features they have in common. Which ones do you think are true or false? Which features do you feel are morally significant? Do you agree with Racy's answers to the above two questions? Be sure to specify the features as you develop your response.

2. If you accept the basic idea of his argument that humans and animals are roughly morally equivalent (note Racy's exceptions), do you think one is therefore committed to: (a) not having pets because they are products of human domestication of what once were wild creatures; (b) vegetarianism, given the taboos on cannibalism; (c) not wearing leather shoes, no matter how good they feel, for they exploit vulnerable and innocent moral creatures; (d) less driving on highways to spare all those bugs that fatally crash into your windshield? Pick one and develop an answer that takes some of Racy's key points into consideration.

65. Bill Shaw, "A Virtue Ethics Approach to Aldo Leopold's Land Ethic"

Whereas Racy emphasizes rights and justice as key to our moral treatment of animals, Shaw believes the virtues are the basis for this moral treatment. He specifies three virtues: respect, prudence, and practical judgment. Only prudence ranks among the classics. Practical judgment is related to prudence, but for Shaw the former implies a more active and sensitive application of prudence.

Although Shaw's account is in part tribute to the thought of Aldo Leopold, I have included mostly his own views as influenced by Leopold. As indicated by the title, Shaw's main contribution is showing how virtue ethics offers the best moral relation to nature. Respect involves an appreciation of how elements in the natural community have a *telos* or fundamental purpose. Prudence embodies the wisdom of "enlightened self-interest" and the understanding of the value of suspending the desires for immediate gratification. Practical judgment combines the first two virtues with the sensitivity one should have for ecological communities and calls for active contribution to the well-being of these communities. Indeed, Shaw concludes, part of this moral shift in applying the virtues involves a shift in the sense of citizenship. Before, we were citizens of a nation-state. Tomorrow, we will be citizens of biotic communities.

Multiple-Choice Questions

1. A bunch of trees in a forest is similar to a couple of human beings insofar as each has the capacity for
   *a. achieving its *telos*.
   b. reproducing through *eros*.

117

c. moral free will.

d. virtuous and vicious deeds.

2. Embracing the land virtues, according to Shaw, is best for
    a. farmers, animals, and tomorrow's children.
    b. people who travel in RVs.
    c. celebrities who need a safe cause.
    *d. everyone.

3. For Shaw, the most important context for humans to weigh moral considerations is
    a. the religious community.
    b. among those who speak the same language.
    c. with other citizens who care to vote.
    *d. the biotic community.

Discussion Questions

1. Why does Shaw pick respect, prudence, and practical judgment as the land virtues? Writers in earlier chapters depicted the virtues in an ongoing struggle with certain vices, such as pride versus humility, or love worried about lust, or justice opposing envy. Which vices do you think the land virtues are most opposed to? Explain your position on this.

2. Near the end of the essay Shaw makes an analogy between the land and slave girls. What is his point in making the analogy? Do you find it persuasive? Why, or why not?

66. William Cronon, "The Trouble with Wilderness"

Much of the dispute about our proper moral attitude toward the environment (including land and animals) has to do with a certain non-moral view of our relation to nature. Are humans basically in charge of their own long-term interests? Or are they part of a larger purpose that they neither understand nor agree on? Is their appreciation of nature a reflection of their own happiness, or do humans respect nature for nature's own well-being?

These questions are investigated by Cronon by reviewing the relatively brief history of how humans have changed their perception of nature. It was only a couple of centuries ago that humans saw nature as wilderness. Nature was, in more contemporary terms, truly Other because it resisted human efforts to understand it and feel comfortable in it. As Cronon adroitly reminds us, pioneers were literally taking their lives into their hands by leaving the comforts of civilization. Wilderness has now become tame, in part thanks to national parks and the growing affluence of Americans who can drive their cars up to grizzly bears and capture the Kodak moment of it staring through the windshield, eyeing the picnic basket or the kids for a possible meal.

Cronon is generally sympathetic with environmental ethics. As a thoughtful scholar, however, he is suspicious of the intellectual grounding that supports this ethics. For, if he is correct, many of the moral beliefs guiding environmental causes rest on sentimental or arbitrary tastes rather than on solid analysis and understanding.

Multiple-Choice Questions

1. Two hundred years ago, when people thought of "wilderness" they did NOT think of
   a. bewilderment.
   b. savage.
   *c. hugging a tree.
   d. barren.

2. Thinking that we can control the purposes or directions of nature is an act of
   a. Congressional authority.
   *b. great hubris.
   c. God's granting us dominion over his kingdom.
   d. scientific authority.

Discussion Questions

1. How does Cronon understand nature as Other? Do you agree with his claim that we have forgotten this perspective? Are there good reasons for changing this perspective? Explain.

2. What does he mean by saying that nature is not just out there but is all around us and even inside us? Illustrate your understanding of Cronon's point by describing an example you have read about or experienced.

67. Josiah Royce, "Loyalty"

The final three essays focus on an intangible object as central to our moral considerations of the other. Royce highlights the virtue of loyalty for two reasons. Loyalty gives an organizing purpose to one's life, and it helps to keep every moral person from succumbing to the preoccupation with individualism that Royce finds rampant in our culture (written early in this century!). The excerpts are from a series of public lectures given by Royce, so you can assign sections separately.

Royce's main concerns are conceptualizing the meaning of loyalty and warning against the loyalty in zealotry that brings more harm than good. His examples of patriotism and the war spirit highlight this concern. On one hand, the loyal person joins the cause and begins feeling a sense that his personal will has suddenly become part of a more powerful will. This experience is both intense and purposeful. On the other hand, there is the danger that it also fosters a fanaticism in which the loyalty of other people's causes is diminished or eliminated, or that the leader one has been obeying selfishly betrays the cause, thus jeopardizing the trust and well-being of the followers. To circumvent these dangers and still hold loyalty as a fundamental virtue, Royce reminds his audience that the loyal person is also loyal to the idea of loyalty. Hence, the loyal person encourages all moral persons to find a cause that gives them purpose and direction. For, as Royce points out, "unless you can find some sort of loyalty, you cannot find unity and peace in your active living." In this way the virtue of loyalty offers the basis for a just and kind life, a personal and social sense of the good.

Multiple-Choice Questions

1. For Royce, patriotism and war offer
   a. the worst forms of loyalty.
   b. about as much insanity as religious zealots.
   c. the chance for loyal people to realize the highest virtue—courage.
   *d. no necessary connection to loyalty.

2. Which is NOT one of the lesser virtues tied to loyalty?
   a. tolerance of other sincere persons
   b. respect for an adversary
   *c. love for the sinner
   d. fair play in sports

3. If people eschew loyalty and try to find life's meaning within themselves, they will find
   a. a rational plan for life.
   b. the fear of death.
   c. their inner conscience.
   *d. their chaotic nature.

Discussion Questions

1. Royce is careful to prevent loyalty from becoming fanaticism or zealotry. How does he discourage the dangers of loyalty, and do you think he succeeds?

2. Royce presented his talks on loyalty in the beginning of this century, when he admits that excessive individualism threatens to rob moral persons of a meaningful life. If Royce were to return to the United States in the end of this century, to what extent do you think he would say Americans have heeded or ignored his message? What evidence can you provide to show that people have or have not embraced the cause of loyalty?

68. Hildegard von Bingen, "Eighth Vision: On the Effect of Love"

Medieval visionary articulates a moral concern for the other that resides in the spiritual realm. In her writings and music Hildegard was a major contributor to moral reflections on the battle between virtues and vices, and hence we gratefully note her influence in the presentation of some of the selections in this anthology. Here she is worried about the evil temptations offered by Satan and his helpers. For the moral struggle is not just an individual one—it involves the human species. Moreover, this struggle encompasses our bodies and souls as well as our earthly and heavenly lives. Wisdom is the key to battling evil, for through wisdom we understand how God presents us with the three main virtues: love, humility, and peace. These virtues not only thwart the powers of Satan, they "direct the spirit . . . toward a longing for higher things."

Multiple-Choice Questions

1. That every human contains something within that moves all sorts of directions indicates that
   a. every human has a good soul.
   *b. each of us has a shadow.
   c. we all have organisms inside our bodies.
   d. everyone is possessed by demons.

2. Which is NOT one of the three key virtues?
   *a. prudence
   b. humility
   c. love
   d. peace

Discussion Questions

1. What are at least three key features of human beings, according to Hildegard? How do these features contribute to efforts in leading a moral and spiritual life?

2. In the opening paragraph Hildegard describes a vision of three splendid forms. Do you find any meaning in this vision?

3. How do you compare her view of humility with other readings on humility? Select two or three readings and develop a comparison.

69. Plato, "Beauty, Truth, and Immortality"

This excerpt from *The Symposium* is included not only for Socrates' encounter with the oracle Diotima, but for Diotima's eloquent lesson to Socrates on how love of the highest good is a divine love, encompassing beauty and truth. In his speech on this love, Socrates tells his friends that the greatest desire is no longer corporeal. Rather, the greatest desire brought about by true love is desire for true knowledge, and in this sense the lover of knowledge seeks immortality.

You have probably covered this dialogue in other courses. Since many students who take introductory ethics may not be taking another philosophy course, I thought including this selection (with Royce and Hildegard, if possible) might offer students a feel for how expansive the vision of philosophy can be. Ethics, in this perspective, is more than asking "Why should I do or not do this?" From Plato and other thinkers' perspectives, ethics also inquires about one's place in the larger scheme of things; or, what is our relation to the mysterious other?

In assigning the selection you might briefly give the background to the dialogue, such as what the earlier speakers had to say about love.

Multiple-Choice Questions

1. As Plato presents it, the gods are not seekers of the truth because
   *a. they are already wise.
   b. they are so powerful that they do not need knowledge.
   c. in ancient Greece the gods were seen as blessing ignorance.
   d. knowledge brought arrogance, which is unbefitting of a god.

2. When a man gazes upon true beauty, then he will
   a. ask for her hand in marriage.
   b. paint its picture so he can have it forever.
   *c. gain perfect virtue.
   d. see the futility of life.

Discussion Questions

1. What lessons does Diotima teach Socrates about the relation between love and immortality? How does this discussion of love compare to other views of love you have covered so far?

2. How many levels of beauty can you identify in Diotima's story? Do all the levels exist, or are they speculative or imaginary in Socrates' view of things? Which levels of beauty do you think most humans appreciate or desire?

3. Near the end of the speech Plato writes, "It will be easy for him to talk of virtue to such a listener, and to discuss what human goodness is and how the virtuous should live—in short, to undertake the other's education." What is meant in this passage? Note its context and your general interpretation of Diotima's story in discussing this quote.

Chapter Review Questions

1. What does it mean to have a moral concern for someone or something that is different or strange to us? Select two or three of the readings to discuss the general meaning of this issue and then cite an example to highlight how this concern applies to ordinary situations.

2. Do you think the caring virtue and environmental ethic are distinct and new, or do you see them as reviving familiar moral values with a modern name? Be specific in your response; cite passages from the appropriate readings to develop your answer.

3. How do the various moral views on the other address the natural tendency to take care of ourselves and seek our own happiness? Select three or four selections and identify what you think are their main points about self-interest and its relation to a moral regard for others.

Chapter 9
The Problems of Burdensome Lives

Unless you are teaching introductory ethics for the first time, you have likely discussed the issues in this chapter and probably reached some confidence in presenting them. (The capital punishment debate could also have been included here, except that under the anger category it has a special role.) Many ethics teachers prefer a problems-oriented approach at either a practical or a normative level. Abortion, treating the elderly, and assisted suicide (or euthanasia) clearly rank among the most pressing moral problems in recent years. That these are dramatic and infrequent problems, that is, not always part of ordinary conduct, does not diminish their significance. Any ethics course that can help students understand the philosophical, moral, and cultural aspects of these issues makes a sound pedagogical contribution. All I have to add here is how a virtue ethics perspective understands these issues. The three selections that emphasize virtue ethics have several purposes. One, they can highlight for students the weaknesses and strengths of other approaches. Two, they can invite students to appreciate how a virtuous person makes a decision in a specific moral dilemma. Three, and perhaps most important, they can initiate a discussion among students about whether a virtue ethics approach or another approach is best equipped to help us do the right thing in a complicated situation. Recent scholarly discussions about virtue ethics generally recognize the importance of cultivating the virtues and avoiding vices in seeking the good life. However, many commentators question whether virtue ethics should be the primary anchor to a moral life. In addition, they doubt that virtue ethics can be complete; that is, however interesting virtue ethics may be, they are not convinced that it is equipped to deal with *all* aspects of understanding and pursuing the moral life. Whereas other chapters in this anthology talk about specific virtues and vices from different perspectives, this chapter offers you the opportunity to assess the full value of a virtue ethics perspective by seeing how it directly addresses widely discussed moral problems. It is quite possible that students will, in the end, prefer a non-virtue ethics–based approach to these and other problems.

Picard's case study evokes the meaning of silence in different ages. This is the only case study of the book that could be read after assigning the other selections in the chapter. That is, there is a kind of silence that should be respected when it comes to talking about who should live and who should die.

The selections on abortion represent recognizable positions. Noonan assumes a fairly traditional Christian belief to say that abortion is *almost* always wrong, given the basic value in life. Thomson's famous essay on the right to abortion relies on several analogies to show that there is nothing inherently evil about ending an unwanted and unintended pregnancy. Sherwin outlines a feminist case for maintaining the legality of abortion, particularly given the political and historical record about men controlling women's bodies and autonomy. Hursthouse describes how a virtue ethics perspective approaches a possible abortion by reminding us of the emotional and moral confusion that a pregnant woman undergoes in such a dilemma.

Callahan's well-known case for setting some socially agreed upon limits on health care for the aging is followed by Purviance's criticism charging Callahan with a misunderstanding of the virtues and their application to the meaning of old age. Interestingly, Callahan's focus is on justice and humility, whereas Purviance talks about happiness, pride, and gluttony for life. A related but distinct moral issue involves assisted suicide (related in empirical sense, given that most of the cases are about the elderly). Quill presents a moving story about helping a (nonelderly) patient end her own life. Bogen outlines some of the considerations made by a virtuous person when confronting a potential suicide.

70. Case Study: Max Picard, "Childhood, Old Age and Silence"

There are always moments when silence arises. But silence can speak volumes. Picard meditates on the meaning of silence in the early and late stages of life. He juxtaposes silence with the Word, usually spoken in a recognizable language, to indicate how silence takes on different functions and values. Here he distinguishes the silence of a child full of life and the silence of the aging couple knowing that their death awaits them. The silence that surrounds death is a major reason I used Picard for the case study. Yet I suspect Picard would not want us to forget the poetic and original silence experienced in childhood.

126

Multiple-Choice Questions

1. Picard says the child's language is poetic because
   a. it rhymes.
   b. children do not like literal language.
   *c. it is first-hand.
   d. of the rich and descriptive content.

2. Children are called "little hills of silence"
   a. as an irony in light of their incessant noise.
   *b. as if they form a conspiracy against all chatter of the adults' world.
   c. because that's the ideal when two or more children are in the same room.
   d. because they are bigger mountains of trouble.

3. When an old couple speaks with one another, it often is like
   *a. a burden that has grown too heavy.
   b. being in love again, for they still enjoy each other's voices.
   c. being nervous about too much silence.
   d. they are worried that the other has tuned out.

Discussion Questions

1. What does Picard mean by silence? Does silence have any positive value? Explain.

2. What's a key difference between the silence of childhood and that of the old? Recounting your memories of childhood and encounters with the elderly (such as neighbors or grandparents), do you agree or disagree with Picard's understanding of silence? Cite an example to support your view of Picard.

71. John T. Noonan Jr., "An Almost Absolute Value in History"

Noonan articulates the complex historical backdrop and philosophical justification for the principle to treat life as sacred. Although he acknowledges legitimate but rare exceptions to this principle, Noonan argues that since we cannot persuasively determine when a fetus is human, we should side on the dignity of individual life and treat the fetus as human. He notes that much of his view stems from a Christian tradition. Yet Noonan presents his case mostly in secular terminology, challenging a nonreligious person to justify the possible and intentional killing of a human organism (excepting the danger that the mother's own life is in jeopardy).

Depending on how thoroughly you plan on covering abortion, Noonan provides a thoughtful start, particularly if you plan on following up with either Thomson or Sherwin. You could also summarize his main points if you want to discuss other issues regarding abortion. The danger with this option is that students who have seen caricatures of religious views are not given a chance to see for themselves how a religious thinker presents a moral argument on a specific problem.

Multiple-Choice Questions

1. Throughout the last five centuries most moralists against abortion made an exception when
    a. rape or incest was involved.
    *b. the mother's life was at stake.
    c. the mother would consent to a procedure to prevent conception.
    d. a fetus was diagnosed as malformed.

2. When Noonan defends the rights of the fetus since "for the Christian community it is the injunction of Scripture to love your neighbor as yourself," the fetus is viewed as
    a. a Christian.
    b. a member of the political community.
    *c. a neighbor.
    d. an extension of your biological self.

Discussion Questions

1. Which parts of Noonan's essay are addressed to religious people, and which parts to nonreligious people? To what extent are the arguments for either audience persuasive? On what grounds can the religious and nonreligious audiences discuss Noonan's points together?

2. Why does Noonan think abortion generally violates the basic moral principle that all human lives are equal? Do you agree or disagree with his case? Cite specific passages to support your response.

72. Judith Jarvis Thomson, "A Defense of Abortion"

If there is good reason to suspect that we can never satisfy all interested parties about the precise status of a fetus, then we need to turn to other approaches in assessing the morality of abortion. Thomson's well-known essay highlights the analogy of a woman with an unwanted fetus to a hospital patient discovering himself the blood source for a famous violinist. Thomson introduces other analogies to make her general case that a woman with an unwanted fetus should be legally and morally permitted to have an abortion. In her view the "right to life" argument has too many flaws to be philosophically persuasive. Thomson acknowledges that some abortions can be judged indecent. If the pregnancy is in the last trimester, and the only problem is an issue of convenience, then it is a decent decision not to abort, but in general the decision to allow an unwanted fetus to be born is not obligatory but a moral deed beyond duty. In this sense, one may be praised for letting a fetus be born, but one should not be morally condemned for opting for an abortion.

I have included the entire essay partly due to its reputation. It was the essay to introduce a new journal, *Philosophy and Public Affairs*, and it appears in a variety of anthologies, for good reason. Thomson presents her case thoughtfully and precisely, thus encouraging the student to engage in careful philosophical analysis. If you are pressed, you could focus on the violinist analogy and Thomson's challenges to one or two of the anti-abortion views.

Multiple-Choice Questions

1. The analogy of the violinist is relevant to the abortion argument because the violinist
   a. plays good music for fetuses to listen to.
   b. plays the kind of music that tempts people's lustful and procreative urges.
   *c. has a kidney ailment and needs a blood transfusion from another human.
   d. is part of an orchestra, just like the mother is part of a family.

2. For Thomson, if a woman has an abortion in her seventh month to avoid delaying a trip, it is
   *a. indecent.
   b. equivalent to infanticide.

c. not good for her health.

d. immoral.

Discussion Questions

1. If you wake up and find someone directly dependent on you for his or her survival, do you think you are morally obligated to help that person until independence is gained? Why, or why not?

2. Thomson does not endorse all cases of abortion. Which ones does she express reservation about, and why? Do you agree or disagree with her exceptions?

73. Susan Sherwin, "Abortion: A Feminist Perspective"

How is a feminist perspective on abortion different from nonfeminist perspectives? Unlike the latter, which focus on abstract and general principles, a feminist perspective takes serious account of the actual concerns of individual women contemplating an abortion. Nonfeminist perspectives interject masculine values such as privacy or choice that do not address the situational needs and interests of many women. According to Sherwin, this discrepancy highlights the importance of discussing abortion as primarily a woman's moral concern.

She elaborates on the meaning of this concern by pointing out the variety of reasons women opt for an abortion. Illness during pregnancy, difficulties at work or home, limited financial resources, a brutal and violent father, chromosomal anomalies discovered in the fetus, and a child's incompatibility with the woman's life plan are among the justifications for seeking an abortion. To degrade the significance of these reasons neglects the fact that we live in a patriarchal society, notes Sherwin, hence anti-abortionists are indirectly encouraging the continued dominance of women by men. Thus the morality of abortion cannot be extracted from its political context. She also devotes an extended discussion to recent studies on fetal medicine, which implies that the fetus is an individual distinct from the mother that harbors it. For Sherwin this too neglects the fundamental fact that "fetuses develop in specific pregnancies that occur in the lives of particular women." Consequently, the morality of abortion cannot arbitrarily shift exclusively to the fetus as if the woman's body is absent.

Multiple-Choice Questions

1. In Sherwin's view, to expect a woman to choose not to have sex with a man
   a. exaggerates the Commandment that forbids adultery.
   *b. overlooks the power of a male culture that deprives women of sexual control.
   c. is silly in light of recent scientific discoveries about the power of hormones.
   d. makes sense if the man has not expressed any love for her.

2. Most groups actively opposed to abortion are, according to Sherwin,
   a. right-wing terrorists who condone the bombing of abortion clinics.
   b. fundamentalist religious groups.
   c. led by men.
   *d. defenders of many politically conservative policies.

3. In response to the adoption option, Sherwin believes
   a. adoption is too risky in light of this country's erratic laws on parental rights.
   b. it has not worked in most parts of the world, so don't expect it to work here.
   *c. that for many women surrendering an infant is more difficult than aborting a fetus.
   d. foster homes are already overpopulated.

Discussion Questions

1. Getting pregnant is not always a result of free choice. According to Sherwin, much heterosexual behavior appears in the form of sexual coercion. This coercion can be physical or emotional. That this coercion is part of a culture in which "women often have little control over their sexual lives" means abortion is one way of alleviating women from the oppression by men. What additional reasons does Sherwin provide for this argument? Can you offer additional evidence to support or weaken her case?

2. What does Sherwin mean by saying that abortion is not only a moral issue but also a political issue? Outline her main points, then consider why you agree or disagree with them. You might weigh two examples. First, what can Sherwin say if a political

131

conservative supports the legalization of abortion? Second, what might her response be if a feminist or political liberal is generally opposed to abortion, except for extreme circumstances such as the mother's life being at stake?

74. Rosalind Hursthouse, "Virtue Theory and Abortion"

How does a virtue ethics perspective contribute to the abortion controversy? Hursthouse expresses disappointment with the direction this controversy continues to take. It is growingly divisive, fostering rancor and ideological confrontations rather than understanding of an important moral topic. Indeed, in spite of their posturing, the major opponents of abortion actually reflect a superficial or narrow-minded attitude for what a pregnant woman goes through when deliberating about an abortion. Virtue ethics, says Hursthouse, can give us a richer and more insightful view of the psychological, emotional, and moral concerns that face a pregnant woman. Although she admits that a virtue ethics approach will not give us an absolute law prohibiting or permitting abortions, it does offer options overlooked by more familiar approaches.

Her main emphasis is on the idea of happiness or *eudaimonia*, the Greek term for the good or flourishing human life that stems from the virtuous life. This idea embraces the notion that there are some goods particular to humans, given their social, emotional, and intellectual capacities. In addition, these capacities change as one goes through life's stages, from childhood to adolescence and adulthood. Hursthouse points out that it is natural for everyone to have a personal interest in happiness. However, there is a point when this interest is excessive and is manifest in selfishness or callousness in regarding the *eudaimonia* that other humans seek. Virtuous persons, women and men, notes Hursthouse, will use this idea of happiness as the framework for making a moral decision about abortion.

I have omitted Hursthouse's discussion of virtue theory; it was fairly long and technical, useful to an upper-level philosophy student but not an introductory ethics student. Still, I think her discussion of abortion illustrates some of the central tenets of virtue ethics so clearly and thoughtfully that her points could apply to other moral problems as well. It probably ranks as the essential essay for this chapter, and one of the essential selections for the book.

Multiple-Choice Questions

1. If the law allows (or forbids) women the right to an abortion, says Hursthouse,
   a. then virtue ethics should abide by it.
   b. a virtuous person should first read the law to see if it applies to her situation.
   c. a virtuous person weighs the *eudaimonia* likely produced by the law.
   *d. it is irrelevant to virtue ethics.

2. To consider an abortion as comparable to an appendectomy
   a. shows a lack of anatomical knowledge.
   *b. is callous.
   c. is reasonable.
   d. reflects the idea that everyone has a right to an opinion.

3. Pointing to our historical and cultural practices of abortion, and even infanticide, is for Hursthouse
   a. evidence that virtue ethics and moral relativism are compatible.
   *b. insufficient evidence that abortion is morally permissible.
   c. a sign that human beings have always been morally confused.
   d. a sign that women have been universally oppressed.

Discussion Questions

1. How do you think Hursthouse would respond to Noonan, Thomson, or Sherwin? Select at least one of the three earlier essays on abortion and note the distinctive features of a virtue ethics approach to abortion. Then consider whether virtue ethics offers a positive or negative contribution to the abortion controversy. Be specific in your reasoning.

2. What does Hursthouse mean by *eudaimonia*? How does this concept play a role in her discussion of abortion? Do you think this concept helps a woman in deciding whether to have an abortion? Why, or why not?

75. Daniel Callahan, "The Value and the Limits of Aging"

Another familiar controversy on the possibility of a burdensome life concerns old people, the elderly, or senior citizens. Whatever name you prefer, everyone is aging. There is a certain point, though, where getting old presents distinct moral questions. What is the meaning and value of being old? How should the elderly and the young be related so that each contributes to the other? At what point must we recognize the mortality in the elderly and prepare for their dying?

Callahan addresses these questions in a selection that clearly cuts into a cultural and ethical rift. "Who decides, and on what basis, the moral value of an aging person?" has been the spark to numerous television themes, legal and financial battles, and, we ought to admit, favorite topics in ethics courses. Callahan challenges the usual ways of talking about the elderly by saying that we need some sort of social consensus about when to morally ascertain the point at which we should no longer extend a person's life by any means possible. Although his position tends to get distorted by charges of widespread mercy killing, Callahan reminds us that his position has an important context. This context involves the meaning of the lives of elderly persons and their relation to the rest of us. Highlighting several key virtues—including those borrowed from Cicero, such as courage, simplicity, and hilarity—Callahan outlines the components of this relation. These components include a social and moral recognition that this relation involves certain natural spans or limits.

If you want to cover the problem of the elderly but your schedule is tight, you could assign any one of the selections and summarize the others. I have tried to include excerpts with some coherence, so that, for example, you could assign "serving the young" or "obligations and virtues" and summarize the other sections to help students become familiar with the intriguing issues that underlie this moral problem.

Multiple-Choice Questions

1. What the aged, and *only* the aged, can provide for the young is
   a. how pathetic the current generation looks compared to when the aged were young.
   b. what the youth missed out on in the elderly's age of virtue and innocence.
   *c. a perspective on the cycle of the generations.
   d. that the good ole' days never existed, and never will.

2. Which virtue is NOT considered as desirable for old people?
   *a. justice
   b. hilarity
   c. courage
   d. humility

3. Which phrase appears in *each* of the three principles that conclude Callahan's selection?
   a. death with dignity
   b. you can't play God
   c. to each his own
   *d. natural life span

Discussion Questions

1. If you agree with Callahan, would you be able to apply his argument to a close relative or friend in terms of setting limits to that person's life? If yes, list Callahan's main points that you support. If not, is your reason based on objective or subjective reasons? Clarify your answer.

2. What does Callahan mean by saying that the elderly have much to contribute to the youth? Is this contribution more of a personal or a social issue? Does a virtuous youth make sure that the elderly can still be engaged in life, or does a virtuous old person insist on his or her positive contributions if given the chance? Which, if any, passages from Callahan help shape your view?

76. Susan M. Purviance "Age Rationing, the Virtues, and Wanting More Life"

Purviance offers a response to Callahan's proposals that questions his understanding of old age and his appreciation of the virtues. She is not convinced that there is or can be a reliable measuring stick to help us know when to set limits. One flaw with the efforts to identify this measuring stick is that it overlooks the virtues of old age that are distinct from the virtues of younger generations. Although Callahan seems to address this, according to Purviance he fails in view of his assumption that old people have similar characteristics. Offering an interpretation of Aristotle that contrasts with Callahan's interpretation, Purviance admits there is a love for life that can turn into a selfish gluttony for staying alive as long as possible. Yet, she observes, there is also a love for life that is excessive in a benevolent sense, for the old person still has something to contribute that is irreplaceable. Unfortunately, knowing this is more often a personal rather than a social experience. What I have gained from my mother or grandmother is different from what you have gained; but if you and I discuss some unknown person's parent or grandparent, we can make all sorts of objective decisions about when to cut off the life-support machine.

There are several ways to present this selection. For argumentative purposes, it directly questions the Callahan position. For another view of how the virtues help or hinder resolving a moral problem, you might highlight for students Purviance's views of old age. If you like to address the dispute about the personal and social dimensions of virtue ethics, Purviance introduces a conflict of the two. "Health care policy should not corrupt people's virtue," she concludes, "but it should not make virtue the standard of merit."

Multiple-Choice Questions

1. The philosopher most important to Purviance's critique of Callahan is
    *a. Aristotle.
    b. Augustine.
    c. Kant.
    d. you, the reader.

2. In opposing Callahan, Purviance concludes that
    a. social policy should dictate virtue ethics.
    b. virtue ethics should dictate social policy.
    c. virtue ethics and social policy should follow principles of economics and justice.
    *d. social policy and virtue ethics are independent moral concerns.

Discussion Questions

1. Callahan lists seven virtues that characterize a moral old person. Which ones do you think Purviance agrees or disagrees with? From other readings or experiences, which virtues or vices do you believe the elderly embody? Can we learn a moral lesson from their virtues and vices?

2. Do you think Purviance addresses the legal or political aspects of treating old age? Although she recognizes a contrast between social policy and personal virtue, do you think her rejoinder to Callahan offers us a practical direction? If so, what is it? If not, can you help Purviance by introducing one? Briefly explain.

77. Timothy Quill, "A Case for Assisted Suicide"

This selection could work as a case study introducing moral views on euthanasia, but I have included it here because Quill's reflections on his care for "Diane" include his own position. Moreover, he suspects many doctors go through similar professional and personal heartaches about how to help someone who is suffering with all medical hope gone.

Some points worth noting. Quill misleads the funeral director regarding the cause of death, mentioning acute leukemia and omitting any reference to suicide. He emphasizes how much a dying patient can teach us while cautioning against expectations of a peaceful death—there is an intense pain that often permeates the dying person's body. And he has long been an advocate of giving patients more say about how they want to handle their dying. They should have a right to die on their own terms, Quill believes.

Multiple-Choice Questions

1. "Diane" is dying from
   a. vaginal cancer.
   b. a history of alcoholism.
   *c. leukemia.
   d. heart disease.

2. Quill told the funeral director that the cause of death was
   a. heart failure during surgery.
   b. suicide.
   *c. acute leukemia.
   d. poisoning from hospital food.

Discussion Questions

1. In light of Quill's introspection and "Diane's" medical condition, do you agree with his moral decision to help her die? If yes, do

you favor a law permitting assisted suicide, with certain restrictions? If no, where do you think Quill's reasoning is faulty? Be specific.

2. Who should determine whether a person can be granted a request for assisted suicide? Should only doctors have the authority to oversee or carry out an assisted suicide, or should a family member or a friend be permitted to assist a suicide?

78. James Bogen, "Suicide and Virtue"

The final two selections address the issue of when a burdensome life becomes one's own. Most people who support the legalization of assisted suicide emphasize an individual's rights to control his or her body, particularly in confronting a fatal illness. Bogen concisely questions this emphasis on individual rights. He does this by introducing virtue ethics as a perspective that challenges the relation between the right to commit suicide and the moral goodness of suicide. He does not morally condemn all suicide, but he does echo Hursthouse's (#74) belief that a virtue ethics perspective offers a richer and more complex understanding of not only the person considering suicide but that person's relations to family and friends. In that sense, according to Bogen, unlike utilitarianism, deontology, or rights theory, a virtue ethics approach is best able to approach suicide as both a personal and a social moral problem. Hence, introducing virtues such as charity, gratitude, and courage and vices such as cowardice and meanness helps us consider the moral options when encountering a potential suicide.

Multiple-Choice Questions

1. If a man has a right to cowardice, then any action stemming from that right
   a. should not be judged.
   *b. can still be morally condemned.
   c. is logical, hence acceptable.
   d. is a sign of courage that one is committed to one's cowardice.

2. If a virtuous person learns that a friend is considering suicide, the person will
   a. check the latest laws on suicide.
   b. review the moral history of suicide.

    c.   weigh only the friend's despair.

*d.   think of the friend's goodness before making a decision.

Discussion Questions

1.   What is Bogen's understanding of the relation between laws and moral goodness? Do you agree with him that rules and codes do not adequately resolve moral problems? Is his emphasis on virtue ethics a preferable alternative? Why, or why not?

2.   Using one of Bogen's examples or your own, develop a scenario in which someone is considering suicide and a virtuous person enlists virtues and vices to approach the situation. Are cowardice and meanness the only pertinent vices? Are courage and charity the major relevant virtues? In your example clarify how a virtue ethics approach can contribute to a moral solution, and whether this contribution is greater than other approaches.

Chapter Review Questions

1.   What do you think the epigraph by Chuang Tzu that introduces Chapter 9 means? Use any of the essays in Chapter 9 to illustrate what the epigraph means.

2.   Abortion, treating the elderly, and assisted suicide are three moral problems that receive scholarly and popular attention. Using the selections in this chapter, or some from Chapters 1 and 2, which approaches these problems do you find most practical? Most moral? You might weigh the value of a virtue ethics approach as compared to, say, a utilitarian, Kantian, religious, or cultural relativist approach.

3.   Given the familiarity of the topics in this chapter, which two or three readings surprised you the most? Did the surprise stem from the examples, the arguments, new ideas, or something else? Did the surprises change your mind? Be specific.

Chapter 10
Philosophy and the Good Life

Talking about morality often brings up issues about our duties and obligations, which laws and rules to follow, how personal sacrifices are needed to combat everyone's selfish tendencies. In other words, people get the impression that ethics has to do with things we have to do rather than with what we want to do. This dichotomy has the unfortunate effect of viewing morality solely as an arduous task.

The readings in this chapter attempt to address this common attitude more carefully. Many of them try to circumvent the egoism/altruism dispute by examining how philosophy seeks to understand in general the good life. Ethics, as a central component of philosophy, has much to contribute to this understanding. One way of anchoring this approach, then, is by not focusing on pleasure or sacrifice but by discussing freedom or leisure. As Plato and Aristotle remind us, the virtuous life depends on free time; the virtuous state is one that offers its citizens leisure. Leisure enables human life to flourish in a way that labor does not. Freedom encourages us to develop our talents, engage in various social relations, delight in thoughts, dreams, and aspirations. Without leisure and freedom we are reduced to a life of servility.

The moral problem of leisure and freedom is what we do with them. As with many issues in these chapters, this is both a personal and a social moral problem. The value of leisure and freedom, according to many thinkers, is an individual matter, of course. Yet they recommend that we address how customs, institutions, and social practices encourage us to enjoy or misuse our free time. Is it a time for indulgence or productivity? Should we do something meaningful in leisure time? Is freedom good for only some of us, or should it be encouraged for all humans? Is freedom a symptom of a good society, and in our free time might we discover not personal goods but the virtues exemplified in other persons? The selections in this chapter address these questions.

Rybczynski's case study reviews some recent disturbances regarding the inability of many people to enjoy leisure time. With the continued emergence of labor-saving technologies and the drastic increase of basic economic indexes, he finds it odd that people do not seem to enjoy their free time. Pascal reflects on a recurring theme that most people treat free time as merely a chance for pleasant diversions. In his eyes, however, the reason behind these diversions is that we fear fundamental concerns such as self-knowledge, mortality, and spiritual life. Franklin echoes these reservations about squandering leisure by reminding young people that time is money; hence, time wasted is money wasted. Sloth, once a candidate for the deadliest sin (see Jordan-Smith, Chapter 3), is reconsidered by Pynchon in light of classic literary figures and current devices, such as the remote-control and VCR. On one hand, sloth indulges other vices in a peculiar way; on the other hand, sloth may not be as bad as its reputation. Another critique of modern life is offered by Gerbner, who suggests that the time Americans spend watching television is more than a silly diversion—it has become our new religion for our secular culture.

Aristotle and Plato outline the significance of leisure in political and philosophical life. For Aristotle, the virtuous state has leisure as one of its goals, since this allows citizens the chance to learn and develop the virtues as well as enjoy life. Plato observes how the very nature of the philosophical task—to reflect and discuss truth—requires leisure. (Hence, the fact that we have courses in ethics is a sign of a good society. Whether students agree is another matter.) Hollenbach believes that much of our free time is directed toward frivolous ends at the cost of being virtuous and responsible citizens. This dereliction of duty threatens democracy for it deprives citizens of the chance to deliberate on the common good. Saeng contrasts Western culture's delight in materialism and consumerism with a Buddhist attitude toward simplicity and idealism. Some blending of the two is necessary, she concludes, if the excesses of Western culture are to be overcome. In his reflections on travels to different cultures, Lingis reflects on encounters with various individuals who exemplify a frequently discussed but infrequently practiced virtue—the virtue in giving rather than receiving.

Although most of the selections in this chapter are fairly short, you probably will not cover all of them. If your students have some background in philosophy, assigning Aristotle and Plato always provides an intellectual background to more recent discussions. Pascal and Franklin offer a slice of the historical shift in the view of sloth. Although both are critical of wasting free time, for Pascal the reasons are mostly spiritual, whereas for Franklin the emphasis is on efficiency and economics. Pynchon might be most accessible to students; he is a stylistic writer and brings the issue of sloth to current developments.

141

Gerbner's piece on television is concise, but he packs many important observations in a few pages. Moreover, since his essay is twenty years old, it might be worth seeing how prophetic he is. If you prefer a contemporary outlook on the social importance of ethics that eludes the ideological slogans about virtues and vices, the Hollenbach selection raises "solidarity" as a new candidate for a virtue that has a common appeal to various political adversaries.

The selections by Saeng and Lingis illustrate, respectively, traditional outlooks on the good life and moments of moral goodness. To what extent their portrayals are at best exceptions that might spice up an ethics course, or their observations of moral persons can be practically embraced by an ethics student, is a question you might discuss with your class. In any event, I consider Saeng and Lingis two of the essential readings in the book.

79. Case Study: Witold Rybczynski, "The Problem of Leisure"

How do people value their free time? Rybczynski concludes his study of a cultural history of leisure by outlining the tensions modern civilization has with it. Many of us have trouble deciding whether we should do something worthwhile or meaningful with the time away from official or necessary work. For many of us leisure time is meant to be devoted to productive activities—the kind of activities that we can brag about to our coworkers after a long weekend or a vacation. For others, notes Rybczynski in citing Chesterton, leisure is the time in which we can do anything we want—even nothing. By deftly interweaving these observations with a feel for a human paradox about free time, Rybczynski invites the reader to consider the following Monday morning ritual: "What did you do on the weekend?" "The usual," we answer, mixing dismay with relief.

Multiple-Choice Questions

1. Citing the psychiatrist Ferenczi, Sunday is a day meant for
   *a. becoming a master of yourself.
   b. serving the master, your Lord.
   c. hustling to the shopping malls by sunrise.
   d. turning to the nearest football stadium and bowing three times.

2. The one who said that leisure is "the most precious, the most consoling . . . the most holy" was
   a. Voltaire.
   b. the Pope.
   c. Freud.
   *d. Chesterton.

Discussion Questions

1. Rybczynski suggests that a typical Monday morning response to "How was your weekend?" is "The usual," in a tone of dismay and relief. What do you think he means by this? In light of your own experiences and observations, do you think he has captured the tension many people feel in terms of having to do something with their free time? Offer a concrete example to support your answer.

2. Concluding the essay Rybczynski asks, "Do we work to have leisure, or the other way around?" How do you think your fellow students might answer this question? What is your answer? In clarifying your response, consider what you feel is the moral importance or danger of work and leisure.

80. Blaise Pascal, "On Diversions"

We realize that Pascal the moral thinker may have been forgotten given his association with the Wager argument for God's existence and computer programs. These brief essays or aphorisms highlight Pascal's view of the earthly life and the weaknesses of human nature. Although the names may have changed, the kinds of diversions Pascal introduces are not much different from the kinds of entertainment many of us engage in today. For him, however, our attachments to diversions are not expressions of stress therapy, self-actualization, taking care of Number One, or some variation of a meaningful deed. Pascal suggests that diversions are humanity's way of ignoring more pressing issues: the mortality of the self, our inability to understand ourselves, and the uncertainty of our faith in a divine existence.

With these aphorisms it is understandable to emphasize Pascal's religious direction. Keep in mind that Pascal believes most humans are also unhappy, and in this sense diversions or little amusements divert us from confronting this fact. Although the length is fairly short, if you want to highlight some passages of Pascal without assigning all of them, you could postpone section #139 and assign the other sections on vanity, happiness, and thinking. Orienting your presentation of Pascal might be based on section #168: "*Diversion.—*As men are not able to fight against death, misery, ignorance, they have taken it into their heads, in order to be happy, not to think of them at all."

Multiple-Choice Questions

1. The happiness of those in high positions, says Pascal, lies in having power and
   a. great wealth.
   b. public honors.
   *c. underlings to amuse them.
   d. a better chance for immortality.

2. For Pascal, diversion is
   a. the only thing that consoles us.
   b. our greatest misery.
   c. either (a) or (b), but not both since they are contradictory.
   *d. (a) and (b), since humans are contradictory creatures.

Discussion Questions

1. Pascal describes diversions as an escape from more pressing questions. What are these questions? How can Pascal or anyone know that another person is engaging in pleasurable activities in order to avoid thinking about these questions? In response, you might consider whether Pascal is inquiring about friends, colleagues, acquaintances, or himself.

2. Pascal raises the perennial question about self-knowledge. Yet he questions not whether it is a good thing but whether most of us are afraid of really knowing ourselves. What are his key reasons in supporting this view, and do you agree or disagree with him? Explain.

81. Benjamin Franklin, "Advice to a Young Tradesman"

This short selection was written over 200 years ago, but aside from terms such as "sixpence" and the spelling of words such as "produced" in several ways, it applies today as much as more contemporary writings. On one hand, Franklin anticipates current attention to the financial emphasis on so many dimensions of ordinary life. Time is worth something, do not waste your time, and have quality time with the kids suggest that time is measurable in a way that corresponds to a monetary calculation. On the other hand, contrary to recent reliance on credit cards and bankruptcy declarations, Franklin admonishes those who engage in credit. To engage in credit is to risk a relation of dependency. To avoid this, he endorses the virtues of Industry and Frugality.

This is the second selection from Franklin. He is considered one of the founding fathers of American democracy and culture in light of his writings, politics, and scientific inquiries. It might be fruitful to ask students to compare their own sense of American life with Franklin's vision.

Multiple-Choice Questions

1. If you borrow money from someone, according to Franklin, you should
   a. pay it back earlier than promised, in case you need to borrow again.
   b. pay it back later than promised, in case the lender forgot.
   *c. pay it back right on time, as you promised.
   d. wait until the lender threatens legal action before you pay it back.

2. Creditors are those who do NOT have the
   a. sharpest eyes.
   *b. greatest personal wealth.
   c. best memories.
   d. keenest ears.

Discussion Questions

1. Do you think Franklin is being literal or rhetorical in his discussion about time being money? Which passages support your interpretation?

2. Franklin notes that industry and frugality are key virtues in attaining happiness? Why does he believe this? Do you think these virtues are the basis for personal happiness and social well-being? In responding to Franklin's essay, consider which passages no longer pertain and which still have something to say to current times.

82. Thomas Pynchon, "Sloth"

The abundance of phrases warning against sloth are part of anyone's childhood. "Lazy bones," "pokey puppy," "early bird catches the worm," "idle hands are the devil's playmates" are among the many reminders that inactivity is more than a physical state—it is a moral issue too. According to Pynchon in his concise historical review, many of our best-known literary works dramatize the dangers and temptations of sloth. Today, with so many labor-saving devices introduced every year, the interest in sloth is just as great as ever.

Pynchon begins by noting how sloth (or acedia) was a candidate for the deadliest vice. He wittily notes that capital punishment for sloth seems excessive, then turns to writers as capturing some of the ambiguities of sloth. Here he introduces some advantages and disadvantages of sloth. Sloth may actually be the time for curiosity, reverie, and reflection. It can also represent apathy, sorrow, and resignation. Finally, he notes the current exemplar of sloth, the couch potato, to highlight how recent technologies facilitate idleness. Yet, Pynchon suggests, somewhat ironically, that channel-surfers or video-game players may be pictures of sloth in our conventional world but in cyberspace they may have transcended acedia and realized a life worth living.

Multiple-Choice Questions

1. Which is NOT one of the meanings of the Latin term "acedia"?
   a. deliberately self-directed
   *b. having an acid tongue and demeanor
   c. loss of spiritual determination
   d. sorrow

2. The present day model of sloth is
   a. people listening to Rush Limbaugh or Larry King on talk radio.
   *b. the couch potato.
   c. a writer who lives on the income of a spouse or family member.
   d. a homeless person or panhandler.

Discussion Questions

1. Find at least three reasons for sloth being a candidate as a deadly vice. According to Pynchon, who is a good historical example

and a current example of sloth? Compare the two examples for similarities and differences.

2. Should sloth still be considered a moral vice? How does sloth threaten personal or social well-being? Can sloth offer some goods to individuals or social relations? Consider some recent developments in the United States, such as the increase of legalized gambling, computer services, network and cable television, or (pick your own). Do these represent endorsements of sloth? Are they moral, immoral, or neutral? Explain your answer, relying on the readings and your own observations.

83. George Gerbner, "Television: The New State Religion?"

It is possible that the omnipresence of television in modern culture is not so much a symptom of sloth but an indicator that the United States (and other technological cultures?) has a new religion. Gerbner outlines his proposal by noting first the salient features of a religious basis of cultural life. These include: a symbolic context to understand and organize reality; rituals, art, science, and political forces that emphasize the larger community; modes of storytelling that range from folktales with moral lessons to legends about the nature of the universe and the meaning of life. During the last several centuries, industrial and democratic forces altered the basis of cultural life. With printing and, later, mass communication forming a new sense of the public, traditional religions diminished in their ability to be a cohesive force in society. What can take their place? Relying on a Marxist framework for articulating this shift, Gerbner suspects only television has the wide-spread and inescapable power to command the attention that was formerly given to religion. In addition to storytelling, symbolic context, universal audience, and vivacity in portraying life, observes Gerbner, "television is truly a cradle-to-grave experience."

If he is correct, is this new religion a blessing or a curse? Should we prefer it to the old religions, or is there still some other basis for culture that we should seek? Gerbner leaves these and other questions for students to consider on their own. Although this essay is fairly short, some of Gerbner's concepts and Marxist perspective might need to be clarified when assigning this to students. Once done, though, this can be a richly rewarding essay, particularly if you can encourage students to assess Gerbner's six chief features of television and update his speculations.

Multiple-Choice Questions

1. Which is NOT one of the chief characteristics of television as a new religion?
   a. It appeals to people of all ages, genders, and races.
   b. A sense of common consciousness and experience is formed by it.
   c. It is part of family life.
   *d. News anchors are the high priests and priestesses.

2. According to Gerbner, the only ones who escape the influence of television are
   a. poor and uneducated people, since they can't afford the advertised products.
   b. members of organized religion, for they already have their faith.
   c. well-educated people who know better.
   *d. those who live outside the television culture.

Discussion Questions

1. Gerbner closes his essay with a list of questions for further research about the nature and power of television. Select any one and answer it in light of your own social and intellectual development.

2. Gerbner wrote this essay over twenty years ago, before the popular emergence of cable television, remote control, and VCRs. Reread his six salient features of television culture. Do the technological advancements since the writing of his essay reinforce or weaken his suspicions that television is becoming the new religion? Explain your reasons for agreeing or disagreeing with his points.

3. If television is the new state religion, is it a good or a bad sign in terms of the moral development of infants, children, teenagers, and adults? Would you recommend another cultural basis? Why, or why not?

84. Aristotle, "Politics, Leisure, and Happiness"

For those who contend that virtue ethics is strictly a personal ethic, and many of the previous selections have not changed your mind, you can always return to this selection from Aristotle's *Politics*. Here he outlines how a virtuous government and virtuous citizens seek leisure and peace, for in this state people have the best opportunity for experiencing happiness. Thus the good life is a combination of morality, reason, and well-being. Although Aristotle acknowledges that external fortune and misfortune play a role in human efforts, virtue is within human control because it can always be taught and practiced. The opposite of the virtuous state is not so much one that is unjust but one that thrives on war. The militaristic state expends leisure time in preparation for battle rather than in enabling its citizens to enjoy peace. Courage, of course, needs to be encouraged to protect the state from invaders. And the other fundamental pagan virtues—wisdom, temperance, and justice—are also central to Aristotle's vision of the proper ends. As he puts it, "If it be disgraceful in men not to be able to use the goods of life, it is peculiarly disgraceful not to be able to use them in time of leisure—to show excellent qualities in action and war, and when they have peace and leisure to be no better than slaves."

Multiple-Choice Questions

1. Which of the following does NOT make men good and virtuous?
   *a. happiness
   b. rationality
   c. nature
   d. habit

2. Leisure is most easily obtained by
   a. having a very powerful monarch.
   b. taking over other countries and making the enemies your slaves.
   *c. practicing the basic virtues.
   d. winning the lottery jackpot.

3. That a good musical performance cannot be attributed to the instrument shows that
   a. happiness is mostly the result of good fortune.
   *b. external goods are not the primary source for happiness.

c.   happiness has nothing to do with the physical world.

d.   believing oneself happy is the same as being happy.

Discussion Questions

1.   What are the key components to happiness? Why does Aristotle think a good government is directly concerned about the happiness of its citizens? Do you agree or disagree with his view?

2.   How is leisure understood by Aristotle? Why is leisure an unlikely experience in a militaristic society? Does Aristotle suggest leisure is the experience of doing nothing at all? Clarify his views on leisure and how it is central to the good life.

85. Plato, "On Free Time and Truth"

The *Theaetetus* is generally known as one of Plato's most thorough discussions on epistemology. Amid the theoretical speculations he interjects a passage in which Socrates sketches several practical conditions for the pursuit of truth. Foremost is leisure. Without leisure one is not only unable to seek the truth, one is not even free.

What is so important about this freedom? It is the basis for philosophical activity. And, depending on whether one devotes a life's task to this activity and becomes a philosopher, this activity is subject to public ridicule. Listen to what Socrates says on the apocryphal story about Thales tumbling in a well because he was looking upon the stars. "Anyone who gives his life to philosophy is open to such mockery. It is true that he is unaware what his next-door neighbor is doing, hardly knows, indeed, whether the creature is a man at all; he spends all his pains on the question, what man is, and what powers and properties distinguish such a nature from any other."

To be unaware of your next-door neighbor hardly seems to be a guide for the moral life. Students curious about the importance of philosophy or an ethics course may wonder about this passage. Being philosophical seems at best amoral. Socrates adds, however, that philosophizing might underscore moral life. Without knowing who we are or what we are not, how can we decide who is moral and why? How can we pursue the good life if we do not know what counts as the good life?

I originally placed this chapter on leisure right after the chapter introducing virtues and vices. Several reviewers questioned this placement, recommending it go at the end instead. I remain unsure whether their reasoning was that leisure was an issue of much lower moral significance or that attention to the good life should be the culmination of an ethics course. In either event, I abided by their judgment. That is why this selection by Plato is here rather than closer to the beginning of the text. In a sense, it is a Platonic version of the case study by Robert Coles on the tension between intelligence and moral goodness. Whether you assign this selection or just summarize it, its key point is one of the most important ones of the text.

Multiple-Choice Questions

1. When the populace encounters the free spirit of the philosopher, the most frequent emotion is
    a. hatred.
    b. jealousy.
    *c. laughter.
    d. love.

2. As portrayed by Socrates and his friends, the lawyer's most noticeable feature is
    a. making lots of money.
    b. being the best conduit to justice.
    c. formal education.
    *d. being a slave.

Discussion Questions

1. How do the people or masses view the philosopher or the philosophical activity? According to Plato, what are the reasons behind the view? In your view, is Plato emphasizing the philosophical person or the philosophical activity when describing how most people view philosophy?

2. Why does Plato think that philosophy requires free time? From your other readings and experiences, do you find that understanding things and seeking the truth are best done when trying to satisfy the demands of others or when you have leisure time? You might consider some of your own experiences in developing your answer to this.

3. Socrates observes that the philosopher is "unaware what his next-door neighbor is doing." What do you think this means,

and does it indicate a moral aloofness or moral concern for human beings? Cite passages to support your response.

86. David Hollenbach, S. J. "Virtue, the Common Good, and Democracy"

Hollenbach recognizes that popular discussion of virtues and vices seems quaint. In his view this is unfortunate because a deeper appreciation of virtue ethics might generate more serious attention to political and social problems. This attention would be focused not so much on more personal issues such as sexual morality or family values but on the idea of the common good. The lack of any significant and popular attention to the idea of the common good provides, in Hollenbach's view, a justification for individual autonomy as the basis for a moral life. To overcome this danger, he proposes two candidates for important virtues: solidarity and mutual responsibility. The relevance of these virtues does not always have to be on a grand or national scale; solidarity and responsibility for one another can be realized in smaller social groups, such as neighborhoods, professions, or colleges. In developing these points Hollenbach addresses several current social problems and the ideas of recent thinkers, especially John Rawls.

Multiple-Choice Questions

1. For Hollenbach, the difficulty in seeing a common good lies in
    a. individual rights.
    b. materialism and capitalism.
    *c. a preoccupation with personal identity.
    d. ongoing factional religious disputes.

2. Committing oneself to a common good, as noted by Pope John Paul II, signals the virtue of
    *a. solidarity.
    b. love.
    c. courage.
    d. prudence.

3. According to Hollenbach, democracy requires the heretofore understated virtue of
    a. universal self-esteem.
    b. rational rather than sentimental self-interest.

    c.   charity to strangers.

*d.   mutual responsibility.

Discussion Questions

1.   If you were the political leader for a day, what would you tell your citizens is the common good? Which passages of Hollenbach would you use to clarify *your* vision of the good that should be on the minds of all citizens? If you are going to introduce notions such as "love your neighbor" or "be just" or "do as you please but don't harm anyone," clarify them.

2.   How practical is Hollenbach's proposal for two new virtues? Outline his main points on this and explain the reasons you support or question his proposal.

87. Chandra N. Saeng, "Insight—Virtue—Morality"

There is always a risk when trying to include non-Western readings. Will they be taken out of context? Are we giving lip-service to major systems of truth and ethics by offering a brief selection or two? However, many of the so-called representatives of the Western canon were or are somewhat out of step with their own cultural context. Socrates was executed; Seneca chose to commit suicide for honor's sake; de Beauvoir has been regarded with suspicion from numerous corners; Bentham insisted in his will that his corpse be present at an annual meeting of great minds; Pascal railed against the mentality of his own times; Daniel Berrigan has been arrested numerous times; and Wendy Kaminer goes on popular talk shows and bemoans the public celebration of sham communities. In other words, I am no longer sure of the relation of an insightful thinker to his or her own cultural context.

That said, Saeng's selection concisely portrays the difference between the obvious fact that Western values of individualism and materialism are penetrating cultures whose ideals appreciate simplicity and the three basic truths of imperfection, impermanence, and impersonality. Whether this contrast must end in a clear-cut victory of one or the other, or whether some fruitful combination of Western and Eastern values can be endorsed to guide us in the future, is outlined by Saeng. Although Saeng avoids drawing out specific proposals, it is worth noting that she believes the successes of Western science and technology have not provided humanity with true happiness and peace. Hence, her observations deserve comparison with Aristotle and Plato, as well as with those who celebrate recent advances in the information age as a harbinger of creative and liberating forms of social existence.

Multiple-Choice Questions

1. According to Saeng, modern industrial societies can be compared with volcanoes
   a. because the chemical composition of volcanoes is analogous to the human body.
   b. because we see volcanoes as violent though in fact they are usually tranquil.
   c. due to the riches spewed forth by each.
   *d. because both seem peaceful but in fact are ready to explode.

2 . The realization of imperfection, one of the three basic truths, brings about
   a. humility.
   *b. compassion.
   c. self-alienation.
   d. a quick trip to the therapist.

3. In Saeng's view, a life of comfort and pleasure is
   *a. not a life of happiness and peace.
   b. a result of leading a virtuous life.
   c. an indicator that life is not fair.
   d. what the Buddha taught us to pursue.

Discussion Questions

1. Do you think Saeng has an accurate or distorted view of Western culture? Cite specific examples, ideas, and readings to illustrate the extent you agree or disagree with Saeng.

2. Avarice or greed is one of the deadly sins. How does Saeng understand the place of greed in American and industrialist cultures? Do you think her version of the three basic truths is sufficient to battle the power of greed? If so, why? If not, what moral truth do you believe can best combat greed? Or, do you think greed is not as bad as its critics claim? Develop your answer.

88. Alphonso Lingis, "Cargo Cult"

This selection has probably been subject to more omissions than any other reading in the text. Despite this editorial free hand, it is one of the essential selections. Although I have omitted Lingis's comments on Aristotle, Kant, and other well-known philosophers, I have retained his reflections on the moral significance of encounters with fairly anonymous figures in remote places. Relatively free of philosophical terminology, the essay still has a rich vocabulary, particularly in its descriptions of experiences with various persons. These persons seem obviously virtuous in light of their capacity to offer something without any expectation of something in return. Is this the virtue of charity, love, justice, or another one of the classics?

Lingis does not spell out his answer. Instead, he invites the reader to reflect on the nature of a moral person and a virtuous deed in light of observing people who have much less or suffer much more than the average introductory ethics student or philosophy teacher. Illustrating these lessons are lepers, beggars, missionaries, and individuals preparing for their corpses to wind up in the Ganges, the holy river.

One way to introduce this selection is by asking students if the articulation of one's deed is essential to the morality of the deed. Another approach is by inviting students to consider when they have been the recipients (or givers) of benevolent deeds for which no equivalent compensation can or should be expected. A third option could be to ask students to select a memorable encounter described by Lingis and offer a moral analysis of it from the perspective of other readings in the text. For example, do his illustrations help define the relation or distinction of virtuous persons and virtuous deeds?

Multiple-Choice Questions

1. In Calcutta, Lingis does NOT encounter
   a. lepers.
   b. dope peddlers.
   c. pimps.
   *d. terrorists.

2. The present for Gopal from Lingis is
   a. a suitcase full of philosophy books.
   *b. a photograph.
   c. a handful of redeemable American Express traveler's checks.
   d. a couple of rare coins.

Discussion Questions

1. What lessons can be learned from Lingis's encounters? Select one or two and describe which virtues or vices are exemplified.

2. Are the virtues momentarily embodied by Mohan, Arun, or other individuals in this selection part of a personal or social morality? That is, does Lingis illustrate moral acts that are too exceptional to be the basis of modern culture? Why, or why not? In your answer, consider whether you believe modern culture is guided by or negligent of the good life.

Chapter Review Questions

1. How do you understand the moral significance of leisure? Select any two or three of the readings to elaborate on your view of the moral value of free time.

2. What do you think is the meaning of the two epigraphs introducing this chapter? How do they fit the discussions in this chapter? Do you believe that the power to give without any expectation of something in return reflects the mind of a fool, a rich person, a saint, or any one of us? Is this power to be encouraged or ridiculed? Explain your answer.

3. Are television and mass communication the end of moral life or the salvation for public virtue? Select two or three readings to develop your understanding of the place of virtue ethics in personal and social well-being. If useful, provide a popular or personal example to help explain your position.